The SSR Handbook

How to
Organize
and
Manage a
Sustained Silent
Reading Program

Janice L. Pilgreen
Foreword by
Stephen D. Krashen

Boynton/Cook Publishers
HEINEMANN
Portsmouth, NH

Boynton/Cook Publishers, Inc.
A subsidiary of Reed Elsevier Inc.
361 Hanover Street
Portsmouth, NH 03801–3912
www.boyntoncook.com

Offices and agents throughout the world

Library of Congress Cataloging-in-Publication Data
Pilgreen, Janice L.
    The SSR handbook : how to organize and manage a sustained silent reading
    program / Janice L. Pilgreen : foreword by Stephen D. Krashen.
        p.   cm.
    Includes bibliographical references and index.
    ISBN 0-86709-462-1
    1. Silent reading—Handbooks, manuals, etc.   I. Title.
LB1050.55 .P55 2000
428.4—dc21
                                                            99-087986

Editor: Lois Bridges
Production coordinator: Sonja Chapman
Production service: Denise Botelho/Colophon
Cover design: Jenny Greenleaf
Manufacturing: Deanna Richardson

Printed in the United States of America on acid-free paper
05   04   03   02   01   00   RRD   1   2   3   4   5   6

———

For my husband, Marty, who was my pillar of support throughout the research, the writing, the ups and the downs; thank you for believing in me and giving so much.

———

For my daughter, Lindsey, who helped in so many important ways; thank you for inspiring me through your love and confidence.

———

Contents

Foreword

Stephen D. Krashen

Free voluntary reading means reading what you want to read, with no book reports, no questions at the end of the chapter, and not having to finish the book if you don't want to. Sustained silent reading provides children with an opportunity to do free voluntary reading in school. Is this a good idea?

Yes. There is overwhelming evidence that free voluntary reading makes a powerful contribution to language and literacy development, and that it helps developing readers beyond the very beginning level improve: It is good for children, teenagers and adults, and first and second language acquirers. It has been shown to work all over the world, including in the United States (Krashen 1993), in England (Hafiz and Tudor 1989), in Japan (Mason and Krashen 1997), in the Fiji Islands (Elley and Mangubhai 1983), in South Africa (Elley 1999), in Sri Lanka (Elley 1999), in Ireland (Greaney and Clarke 1973), in Singapore (Elley 1991), and Hong Kong (Tsang 1996). (There is a website that provides more information on "extensive reading" in many countries: http://www.kyoto-su.ac.jp/information/er/index.html>).

As Jan Pilgreen points out in this book, a number of studies have been done comparing SSR to traditional language arts instruction, and SSR has emerged as a consistent winner. This research goes back a long way. The first controlled study I was able to find in my review was published in 1948 (Sperzl 1948), and eleven years before that, a study was published showing that children who participated in a self-selected reading program for three years showed excellent gains (Boney and Agnew 1937). Table 1 summarizes the results of controlled studies, studies in which students in a comparison group doing traditional skill-building exercises are compared to children in SSR, with both groups tested on standardized tests of reading comprehension.

Table 1
Tests of Reading Comprehension

DURATION	POSITIVE	NO DIFFERENCE	NEGATIVE
Less than 7m	5	13	3
7m – 1 yr	3	8	0
More than 1 yr	8	1	0

Positive = students in SSR outperform comparison students

Clearly, when studies are allowed to run for a sufficient length of time, those who do SSR do better. (Those who have seen SSR programs understand quite well why short-term programs may not work: students need time to find something to read.)

Note that even a finding of no difference is meaningful: Since students find SSR more pleasant than skill-building activities, if there is no difference we are at least making their lives better. My hunch is that teachers also enjoy SSR time more than skill-building activities.

Warwick Elley's studies give us some idea of the kind of progress children can make with free reading in school. Children in the Fiji Island study (Elley and Mangubhai 1983) were taking English as a foreign language for thirty minutes per day. EFL in Fiji begins in kindergarten, but Elley and Mangubhai focused on grades four and five. The children were divided into three groups: One group had the traditional audio-lingual method, a method that uses a great deal of skill-building via grammar exercises and correction. A second group did SSR. The children read for pleasure for 30 minutes a day. The program closely followed the principles Jan Pilgreen describes in this book: There was access to books, book appeal, encouragement to read, no accountability, and distributed reading time. A third group did "shared reading," in which books of interest were read to the children, with children gradually joining in the reading, then the books were discussed with the children. Shared reading uses "big books" with texts large enough for all the children to see.

The results were spectacular. After two years, students in the two groups that engaged in real reading grew at twice the rate as the audio-lingual students in reading comprehension. In addition, they were better on tests of grammar, word recognition, writing, and vocabulary.

In 1991, Elley replicated these results in Singapore: After three years, children in a "book flood" group who had access to high-interest story books, and did language experience and shared book experience, clearly outperformed comparison children on a wide variety of tests of English.

Elley's most recent study (1999) examines the effect of introducing books into classrooms in Sri Lanka and South Africa, areas in which very little reading has been available to the children. Once again, the results were dramatic. Table 2 presents some results from the South African study. Starting at grade 1, READ classrooms received 60 books, with 60 more available in sets of six titles. Teachers were encouraged to read aloud to the children and silent reading time was provided. As shown in Table 2, children in the READ groups outperformed comparison children in reading comprehension; the results held for groups of children in different provinces, and the gap between the readers and nonreaders increased each year.

SSR studies are not the only evidence we have that free reading works; they are a small part of the picture. There are also a sizable number of correlational studies, studies showing that those who read more do better in every aspect of literacy tested. Here is a recent example from the field of foreign language acquisition: Stokes, Krashen, and Kartchner (1998) tested students of Spanish as a foreign language on their knowledge of the subjunctive. The ONLY significant predictor was how much pleasure reading in Spanish the students had done: the amount of instruction in general, the amount of instruction specifically on the subjunctive, and length of time spent in Spanish speaking countries did not count. But reading counted.

In addition to correlational studies, strong evidence confirming the power of reading comes from case histories of readers. There are many cases of those who credit their high levels of literacy development to free voluntary reading. The novelist Richard Wright, who struggled to get access to books, concluded:

> I wanted to write and I did not even know the English language. I bought English grammars and found them dull. I felt that I was getting a better sense of the language from novels than from grammars. (Wright 1966, 275)

Table 2
Reading Tests Scores for READ and NON-READ Pupils

	STD 3		STD 4		STD 5	
PROVINCE	READ	NON-READ	READ	NON-READ	READ	NON-READ
Eastern Cape	32.5	25.6	44.0	32.5	58.1	39.0
Western Cape	36.2	30.2	40.4	34.3	53.0	40.4
Free State	32.3	30.1	44.3	37.1	47.2	40.5
Natal	39.5	28.3	47.0	32.3	63.1	35.1

Note: Standard 3 = grade 4; (from Le Roux 1996)

Malcolm X became a reader in prison:

> Not long ago, an English writer telephoned me from London, asking questions. One was, "What's your alma mater?" I told him, "Books." (El-Shabbez 1964, 179)

There are also impressive case histories in second language acquisition. Cho (Cho and Krashen 1994, 1995a, 1995b) reported on a group of adult ESL acquirers who had studied English extensively in Korea and had lived in the U.S. for several years, but who reported severe difficulty in using English. Cho introduced them to the Sweet Valley High series. Starting with Sweet Valley Kids (written at the second-grade level), the women became fanatic Sweet Valley readers, gradually moving up to the adolescent series and eventually on to regular romance novels. They reported enjoying the reading enormously, made impressive gains on tests of vocabulary, and reported great improvement in their English. Their friends noticed the improvement and thought they were taking ESL classes: All they were doing was pleasure reading.

Lomb Kato, possibly the world's greatest polyglot (17 languages!) gives free reading the credit for much of her language acquisition achievements, and points out that books are not only effective, they are convenient:

> A book can be put in our pocket, it can be thrown away, we can write in it, we can tear it, lose it, and buy it again . . . we can read during breakfast, after we wake up, and we don't have to phone it when we don't have time to read (unlike working with a private teacher) . . . we may be bored with it, but it is never bored with us. (Cited in Krashen and Kiss 1996)

Why does free reading work so well? Interestingly, both camps in the "reading wars" appear to support it. It has been pointed out that data on the success of free reading is consistent with the Comprehension Hypothesis, the idea that we "learn to read by reading," or, more generally, that comprehension of messages is the essential ingredient in the development of language and literacy (Krashen 1994, 1999). Those who support the view that language and literacy develop through "skill building," that is, through learning rules consciously and practicing them until they are "automatic" also support free reading: It is a fine chance for developing readers to "practice their skills."

We thus see overwhelming research support for free reading and sustained silent reading, and no theoretical barriers. All that remains now is for Jan Pilgreen to tell us how to do it.

Works Cited

Boney, C., and K. Agnew. 1937. "Periods of Awakening or Reading Readiness." *Elementary English Review* 14: 183–87.

Cho, K. S., and S. Krashen. 1994. "Acquisition of Vocabulary from the Sweet Valley Kids Series: Adult ESL Acquisition." *Journal of Reading* 37: 662–67.

———. 1995a. "From Sweet Valley Kids to Harlequins in One Year." *California English* 1 (1): 18–19.

———. 1995b. "Becoming a Dragon: Progress in English as a Second Language Through Narrow Free Voluntary Reading." *California Reader* 29: 9–10.

El-Shabbaz, E. 1964. *The Autobiography of Malcolm X*. NY: Ballantine Books.

Elley, W. 1991. "Acquiring Literacy in a Second Language: The Effect of Book-Based Programs." *Language Learning* 41: 375–411.

———. 1999. *Raising Literacy Levels in Third World Countries: A Method That Works*. Culver City, CA: Language Education Associates.

Elley, W., and F. Mangubhai. 1983. "The Impact of Reading on Second Language Learning." *Reading Research Quarterly* 19: 53–67.

Greaney, V., and M. Clarke. 1973. "A Longitudinal Study of the Effects of Two Reading Methods on Leisure-Time Reading Habits." In *Reading: What of the Future?* edited by D. Moyle, 107–14. London: United Kingdom Reading Association.

Hafiz, F., and I. Tudor. 1989. "Extensive Reading and the Development of Language Skills." *English Language Teaching Journal* 43: 4–11.

Krashen, S. 1993. *The Power of Reading*. Englewood, CO: Libraries Unlimited.

———. 1994. "The Input Hypothesis and Its Rivals." In *Implicit and Explicit Learning of Languages*, edited by N. Ellis, 45–77. London: Academic Press.

———. 1999. *Three Arguments Against Whole Language and Why They Are Wrong*. Portsmouth, NY: Heinemann.

Krashen, S., and N. Kiss. 1996. "Notes on a Polyglot." *System* 24: 207–10.

Mason, B., and S. Krashen. 1997. "Extensive Reading in English as a Foreign Language." *System* 25: 91–102.

Sperzl, E. 1948. "The Effect of Comic Books on Vocabulary Growth and Reading Comprehension." *Elementary English* 25: 109–13.

Stokes, J., S. Krashen, and J. Kartchner. 1998. "Factors in the Acquisition of the Present Subjunctive in Spanish: The Role of Reading and Study." *ITL: Review of Applied Linguistics* 121–22: 19–25.

Tsang. W.-K. 1996. "Comparing the Effects of Reading and Writing on Writing Performance." *Applied Linguistics* 17/2: 210–33.

Wright, R. 1996. *Black Boy*. NY: Harper & Row.

Acknowledgments

The SSR Handbook has been an ongoing project ever since the original pilot study was conducted with my wonderful group of high school ESL students—and so many educators who wanted to know the how-to of SSR program planning and implementation started asking important questions that needed to be answered.

I thank Stephen Krashen for being the consummate mentor and friend, who provided constant encouragement, guidance, and feedback throughout the two-year development of this handbook—and who knew it was an important project to complete, and kept me at it.

I thank Lois Bridges, my editor, who helped me stay focused when my perspective became blurry; offered advice when I wanted it and praise when I needed it; and always maintained her sense of humor, even when "deadlines" came and went.

I thank Barry Gibbons, my colleague and statistician, for his expertise in educational evaluation; his patience and tact when we faced roadblocks; and his wry commentary, which enabled us to laugh when we needed to.

I thank my colleagues and graduate students in the School of Education at the University of La Verne, who offered continuous support and motivation, and graciously understood the times when I became reclusive and tunnel-visioned.

I thank my good friend and professional partner, Karen Russikoff, who supplied much appreciated insight, encouragement, and companionship from the inception of this book through its completion.

I thank the many dedicated classroom teachers who took the time to relate so many interesting, inspirational, and often humorous anecdotes about their personal SSR experiences and made the collecting of authentic information an enjoyable and enlightening process.

I thank the staff and administrators at the Home School and the Community School, who made the research study possible, showed immense professionalism during the conducting of it, and wanted to learn all they could about helping students to become better readers and lifelong learners.

I thank Sandra Mendoza and Albert Medina, my caring and insightful instructional assistants, who worked with our ESL students, helping them to find just the right books and to see SSR as sacred—and who took on many additional responsibilities when I was involved with the analysis of the data.

I thank Marj Anderson, her instructional assistants Lucia Vidal and Hanriet Aghajani, and her ESL students at Glendale High School, who invited us to visit their classroom and shared the joys—and photo opportunities—of SSR with us.

And finally, I thank all of the high school ESL students with whom we worked, who represent a unique blend of special personalities that we will never forget, and whose perspectives we will always be grateful for having shared.

Introduction

Expanding the Vision: Sharing the "How-To" of Sustained Silent Reading

Until I came to this class, I was never able to read a whole book before. I always started to read and then got bored. But when everyone else in class was reading at the same time, I learned how to keep reading. I feel like I'm a pretty good reader now.

Raymond, eleventh grade ESL student

When I first started planning the curriculum for my high school ESL reading classes, I was excited—and extremely naïve. I had a vision that I could offer young people the strategies they needed to read more effectively in their content-area classes—and to do better in school, in general. Our high school hadn't offered any reading programs for the previous ten years, and I thought the students would be as pleased as I was that we were developing new courses to help them read more fluently. I didn't realize how little value most of them placed on reading. I was surprised to find that they simply could not relate to my own zest for it. Students told me frankly that they had been placed in my class because they were poor readers; and as far as they were concerned, taking the class was just a way for them to earn elective credits.

So, on the first day of class when I explained that we would all be reading silently for the first fifteen minutes of class time each day, I literally heard groans. My students asked me how many book reports they would have to do and how many pages of required reading would be assigned each week. I was stunned.

As the semester got underway, the students relaxed, and they began to talk to me. They told me that they had never viewed themselves as strong readers. They shared with me their strategies for getting by in school without really reading much at all. Most of all, they were in awe of the fact that I actually liked to read and wondered how I had come to enjoy it. Spurred on by their interest in my personal reading history, I began to tell them stories about my family's summer vacations. My brother and I would buy ten comic books each and then read and trade them as we drove thousands of miles to whatever vacation spot my parents had picked that year. We didn't want to look at scenery; we wanted to read about Archie and Batman and Richie Rich. Then, at home, in the wee hours of the morning, I devoured teen romances and mysteries under the blanket when I was supposed to be sleeping. The trusty battery in my flashlight gave me hours of uninterrupted pleasure-reading time after the busy events of my day and the hectic homework schedule that I usually followed. My students couldn't believe that I had started out reading comic books and series books like *Nancy Drew* and *Little House on the Prairie.* We talked a great deal about how reading something enjoyable can lead to more reading—and how more reading leads to better reading.

One of my students, Raymond, was the most nervous about being placed in a reading class. He was quiet, shy, and afraid of being ridiculed in front of his peers. He told me that reading aloud in school was one of the worst experiences of his life. In history, he was told to read current events articles at the podium; in science, he was asked to stand up at his seat and read lab reports. Whenever he read, he was mortified as he heard his audience laughing at the slow and halting way he pronounced the words. I explained to Raymond that he wouldn't have to do any reading aloud at all if he didn't want to. I also reassured him that he would have many opportunities to read whatever he wanted . . . *silently.*

Ironically, Raymond was the one who became the most intensely "hooked on books" of all of my students during the three years that he stayed in my class. When he graduated from high school, I gave him a copy of *The Shining*—a book he told me he had wanted to read since he first saw the movie. I could honestly say that from the beginning of his sophomore year to the end of his senior year, this young man had progressed from reading the *Lion King* to reading Stephen King. What was it that caused this momentous change in Raymond and so many others in my classes? It was the opportunity to be involved in an effective Sustained Silent Reading program.

In an inspiring book called *The Reading Environment,* Aiden Chambers (1996) talks about some of the things that make up the "social context of reading." They include where we read, having the books we want, the time we have, whether we're interrupted, our general attitude toward reading, and the reasons we read. Taken together, they form what he calls the "reading environment." Chambers' point is that if we want to be skillful in helping young people to become "willing, avid, and—most important of all—thoughtful readers," we need to know how to create a reading environment that enables them (1). I believe that such nurturing environments can be created within the contexts of effective Sustained Silent Reading (SSR) programs.

Briefly defined, SSR is a short time-span of approximately fifteen to twenty minutes during school when students are allowed to read whatever they like. SSR programs can be offered at virtually any grade level, and many teachers whom I know have experienced a great deal of success with them. However, the truth is that it takes a great deal of time, effort, and know-how to put a successful SSR program into operation. I first recognized this when I was a beginning junior high school teacher almost twenty-five years ago. Though some of my students were happy to be allowed to select books that they liked and even happier to be given the time to read them during class, many others remained unengaged and never truly got into the mainstream of the reading experience. I knew that there must be ways to improve the implementation of my SSR program, but I wasn't sure what they were.

Years later, when I returned to graduate school at the University of Southern California, I began analyzing a large sample of SSR studies to determine what made them effective and found that a pattern emerged: The successful programs shared in common eight particular components. By systematically examining these components in each effective program and determining how they were incorporated, I was able to identify the optimal conditions for strong SSR programs. I now call these components the Factors for SSR Success.

From my experience and my reading, I learned that effective SSR programs do not simply happen by giving students time to read in school. In fact, only when teachers follow specific guidelines do these programs achieve their full potential. At the high school where I worked (and with the same group of students of which Raymond was a part), I decided to create the "ideal" SSR program for intermediate English as a Subsequent Language (ESL) students. My task was to figure out how to follow the guidelines to build in the eight factors that would guarantee our success.

At the same time, another high school in our district made the decision to offer students SSR time each day. The teachers from this school had attended a presentation by Stephen Krashen, who encouraged them to provide in-class time to read. However, having no knowledge of the eight factors, the staff members implemented the program in the only logical way. They simply asked students to "read anything for fifteen minutes." Unfortunately, they ran into numerous problems associated with not being able to keep the students actively engaged in the reading process.

The result was that the students at my school outperformed the other school in four areas: reading comprehension, positive attitudes toward reading, frequency of outside (at home) pleasure reading, and use of a wider range of reading sources. When I shared these findings with the other school's staff members, they appreciated having the new information and immediately began to incorporate the eight

Factors for SSR Success into their own program. Since that time, both schools have experienced the positive benefits of SSR and continue to offer outstanding programs to their students.

Today, I am a teacher educator at the University of La Verne in Southern California and am fortunate to work with many wonderful credential and master's degree candidates who are interested in learning how to implement SSR programs. I also give many staff-development presentations and workshops at a wide variety of schools where teachers and administrators feel they need more than the reassurance that SSR really works. They want "how-to" methods for developing viable programs that motivate their students to become hooked on reading. Even at conferences, I am approached by motivated but frustrated educators who want to know where they can find information on how to set up effective SSR programs at their schools. They pose a variety of excellent questions, all of which I can now answer more easily, based on reading the literature, doing the research, and having direct experience with the eight factors. This widespread enthusiasm for SSR reinforces what I have known for a great while: It is time to stop telling people *that* SSR works and start telling them *how* it works. And that's what this handbook is all about.

1

SSR: Its Roots and Rationale

Having been a secondary school teacher for more than two decades, I confess that I started offering SSR to my students in English classes during my first year of teaching. However, I made this decision solely on the basis of intuitive evidence. I followed what I considered to be a common-sense notion—that students get better at reading by reading.

It was only as I became a more seasoned teacher that I began to search for a stronger rationale to support SSR. I wanted to be able to establish a clear premise, based on research, for providing students with several minutes of instructional "free reading" time each day of the week, five times a week. My first step was to find out as much as possible about the origins of SSR programs. The second step was to see what advantages they could offer our students. Our high school had just allocated funds to develop ESL reading classes, and it was important to be able to justify a wide-scale effort to implement SSR as a main part of the curriculum.

The Roots of SSR

As I began my investigation, I learned that in-school free reading programs are not a new idea. In fact, they have existed since the advent of Individualized Reading in the 1950s and 1960s and have been labeled in a wide variety of ways: Free Voluntary Reading (FVR), Self-Selected Reading, Sustained Silent Reading (SSR), Uninterrupted Sustained Silent Reading (USSR), Sustained Quiet Reading Time (SQUIRT), Drop Everything and Read (DEAR), and High Intensity Practice (HIP). More recently, other unique names have been chosen by schools, such as Positive Outcomes While Enjoying Reading (POWER), selected by junior high school students in Canyon Country, California; and Fun Reading Every Day

(FRED), developed by the students at a middle school in Burbank, California. When students create the names themselves, they feel a strong sense of investment and ownership in their SSR programs.

While some of the components of these programs vary, what they all share is a common objective: "to develop each student's ability to read silently without interruption for a long period of time" (McCracken 1971). As it was originally conceptualized (Hunt 1967, Petrimoulx 1988), SSR was based on six guidelines: (1) the students read self-selected materials silently; (2) the teacher models by reading silently at the same time: (3) students select one book, magazine, or newspaper to read for the entire time period; (4) a timer is set for a prescribed, uninterrupted time period; (5) no reports or records are kept; and (6) the whole class, department, or school participates.

To define SSR, we must first consider the term Free Voluntary Reading (FVR), which refers to any in-school program where part of the school day is set aside for reading (Krashen 1993). It is the umbrella term under which the other in-school reading programs fall. Two types of Free Voluntary Reading are Self-Selected Reading and SSR.

The difference between these two programs is that Self-Selected Reading may incorporate some accountability measures such as student-teacher conferences. As students meet with their teachers, they discuss difficult vocabulary or concepts from their books; read aloud parts of their books to the teacher or engage in retells; or summarize their reading in ways that enable the teacher to monitor their comprehension.

Some Self-Selected Reading programs today are reminiscent of the Individualized Reading (sometimes called Personalized Reading) programs that existed in elementary schools during the 1950s and 1960s. In Individualized Reading the teacher provides the students with quiet reading time, and then reading conferences take place with individual students. Not all students can be involved in conferencing on a daily basis, so those who are not included on a particular day continue to read during the specified time until it is their turn. The teacher then organizes groups to discuss common interests or to tackle common reading problems identified during the conferencing time. Also, a record is kept of each student's problems, interests, and scores on reading assessments (Greaney 1970). In this kind of program, some of the original SSR guidelines are violated. First, there is an emphasis on accountability. Second, it is necessary for the teacher to conference with one student while others are reading, so teacher modeling is impossible, and the silent, uninterrupted aspects of the program are lost.

SSR, on the other hand, does not include any accountability measures, and the teacher does not do prescribed follow-up activities to meet students' skill needs. Book reports, quizzes, and comprehension checks are avoided in favor of simply allowing students to enjoy what they read. And, while the students read, the teacher reads, too. One researcher notes that SSR has been around for as long as people have been reading, remarking that "whenever people select something to read for their own purposes, spend more than a few minutes reading it and comprehending whatever they want, SSR is occurring" (Manning-Dowd 1985). As we will see, however, developing the optimal situation where all students have books they want to read and have a supportive environment to read them in requires some real planning and commitment on the part of the adults involved with the program.

SQUIRT, DEAR, and other such acronyms are simply other terms for SSR (Clary 1991). In these programs, implementation can take place on any scale: in single classrooms; in one school; or throughout an entire district, where everyone— teachers, administrators, and classified staff members—stop what they are doing and read at a particular time for a specified length of time (Moore, Jones, and Miller 1980).

High Intensity Practice, or HIP, is a term unique to studies done by Oliver in the 1970s. HIP programs include SSR, SSW (Sustained Silent Writing), and SSA (Self-Selected Activities). In the SSR portion, the original six McCracken guidelines are incorporated, while SSW offers students chances to write whatever they wish for a given length of time without having to show their work to the teacher. The SSA period permits the students to engage in any activity that involves active response to words—reading, writing, studying, or doing content-area classwork (Oliver 1970).

Whatever term is used for free reading programs, they have gained renewed attention as a promising instructional component in school programs. In some cases, they form part of the regular language-arts curriculum, and in others they operate separately in content-area classes or on a school-wide or district-wide basis.

The Research Base

Once I had an overview of free-reading programs, I sought to find a clear rationale to justify implementing them. I wanted to learn the range of positive outcomes teachers could expect as they created such programs.

First, I discovered that there are two primary reasons why educators have been interested in developing free reading programs at various levels of involvement. One is that they have hoped to see an increase in students' reading achievement (and, of course, corresponding reading test scores). The other is that they, along with various parent groups, have perceived that student motivation to read, in general, is often lacking.

Though how well our students actually read has always been the subject of debate, the emphasis on students' reading achievement has been particularly strong since the release of America's National Assessment of Education Progress (NAEP) reading scores. The circular question people may ask is whether readers are more proficient because they read so much or whether they read so much because they are better readers. Originally, when free reading was incorporated into early programs after World War II, its purpose was to allow students to have the drill and practice necessary to learn to read. It was thought that students needed a special time period to apply and transfer the isolated skills learned during the regular instructional period or reading group (Jenkins 1957, Lawson 1968, Oliver 1970, Mc-Cracken 1971). However, with the influence of work by cognitive psychologists, sociolinguists, and psycholinguists, reading came to be viewed not simply as an act of decoding the print on the pages but as a process requiring a meaningful transaction between reader and text (Pearson 1994). The idea that students who read a great deal tend to become better readers gained prominence, along with the notion that the best way to develop reading ability is not through isolated skill and drill practices, but by reading itself. This view of reading—with its highly personalized, meaning-making emphasis—has been stressed by Smith (1988a, 3):

> The purposeful nature of reading is central, not simply because one normally reads for a reason . . . but because the understanding which a reader must bring to reading can only be manifested through the reader's own intentions.

The role of the reading teacher is to ensure that learners see adequate demonstrations of reading for meaningful purposes and help them fulfill similar purposes themselves.

Similarly, Krashen's (1988) research indicates that in-school free reading programs show outstanding results in promoting the development of reading comprehension. His hypothesis, that genuine reading for meaning is far more valuable than doing workbook exercises, evolves from the belief that children learn to read by reading. Arguing that free reading is the "missing ingredient in language arts, as well as in intermediate second and foreign language instruction," he identifies it as the bridge between a basic foundation in a language and higher levels of proficiency (1993, 1). These findings are supported by Elley's (1992) study of twenty-seven countries, in which a steady trend upward in achievement was seen in the populations which engaged in the greatest amount of free voluntary reading.

When we lament that students are not reading well enough, what we often mean is that they aren't reading avidly. Many students know how to read enough to get along in school but have not become independent readers (Allington 1975, Sadoski 1980). Despite teacher encouragement, it is a fact that many students do not read much outside of school (Moore, Jones, and Miller 1980, Watkins and Edwards 1992). We do not see them zealously taking pleasure reading books home or visiting the school or community libraries. They do not spend much time at home engaged in what we would call a "good book." Younger children may not have books readily available, a quiet place to read, or adult role models to help them foster a desire to read. Junior high (or middle school) and high school students often have additional demands placed upon them due to organized sports, peer group activities, homework, part-time employment, and social commitments. Of course, there are also the enticements of television, video games, and computers. These activities all tend to decrease the amount of leisure time that students have to pursue their own reading. For these reasons, "They need to be guided into a situation where reading is respected, quiet is expected, and the students see each other and their teachers in a productive and enjoyable reading environment" (Cline and Kretke 1980, 504).

Also, in order for children to be prepared to read for enjoyment and information, they must learn to be independent in making book selections and setting purposes for reading. We can help students begin to achieve this autonomy by surrendering some control to them. To do this we must provide them with opportunities to read under conditions in which they choose their reading selections, their purposes, and their own demands for learning. This is why they need carefully-orchestrated periods of time to read in school.

As Barbe and Abbott (1975) explain it, school programs must help children learn to read, and equally important, help them to grow into adulthood, loving books and continually "enriching their lives and the lives of others by what they have found on the printed page" (20). Because reading is intrinsically rewarding, it induces students to develop the book habit, which represents a positive, long-term effect. In fact, in one longitudinal study, students who had participated in a free reading program in their school were reading more books—as many as six years later—compared with their counterparts from the comparison school in which no free reading program was offered (Greaney and Clark 1975).

In an effort to see more clearly the range and results of free reading programs that have been developed over the past several decades, I surveyed the literature and found thirty-two free reading studies in which the goals included (1) an increase in student reading comprehension or achievement and (2) improvement in student motivation to read. (See Appendix A for a reference list of these studies.) My purpose was to read each study and determine which groups were successful with respect to these two goals. I could then highlight and use the common components to develop other optimal SSR programs.

Within the thirty-two studies, there were forty-one experimental groups that were engaged in free reading programs. Of these, ten were successful in attaining statistically significant results in reading comprehension; seven were successful in attaining statistically significant results in reading motivation; and fifteen were successful in attaining "observable" growth in reading motivation—that is, improvement which could be quantified but not interpreted through the use of inferential statistics. (See Appendix B for a listing of the studies, the groups, and the results.) For each experimental group that reached statistical significance, a comparable control group operated; in the case of the groups that made only observable growth, there were no control groups. Interestingly, in the cases where the experimental groups did not do significantly better than the control groups, they did just as well, with the exception of two groups. And, in these two groups, where various combinations of SSR and skills were used, the amount of actual SSR time was not possible to calculate. Based on these results, I was able to conclude that SSR provided at least the same or better benefits for students in the areas of comprehension and motivation as traditional skills classes did. This is an astounding finding, particularly when we consider which alternative is more enjoyable for students. Clearly, free reading is less work than skill and drill and a good deal more fun.

To see specifically what elements the successful programs included, I analyzed them and discovered that they shared eight Factors for SSR Success. These factors include the following:

1. access
2. appeal
3. conducive environment
4. encouragement
5. staff training
6. non-accountability
7. follow-up activities
8. distributed time to read

Though not every successful group included each factor, six of the factors were incorporated the most consistently: access to books, book appeal, conducive environment, encouragement to read, non-accountability, and distributed time to read. The two factors which were not included as regularly were staff training and follow-up activities, and I will mention possible reasons for these gaps when I discuss them separately in Chapter Two. However, these results do not suggest which factors are more important than others. They only show the general trends that emerge, overall, when many of the factors are faithfully included in free reading programs (See Appendix C for a breakdown of groups by percentage that included each factor.)

If someone had pinpointed the eight factors for me before I began my work, I probably would have thought they were obvious, or at least based on commonsense expectations. As it turns out, only four of the factors are related to the "rules" initially identified by McCracken: *appeal*, which includes self-selection of materials; *conducive environment*, which includes uninterrupted time for all students; *en-*

couragement, which includes teacher modeling; and *non-accountability*, which includes no required reports or records. Four factors, however, are entirely new ones, which I discovered as an outgrowth of the review of the SSR studies and can now define comprehensively: *direct access to books, staff training, follow-up activities*, and *distributed time to read*. (And, in relation to the original factors, the studies I analyzed led to the development of broader definitions than those provided by the earlier McCracken work.) Even as a veteran teacher with a hefty number of teaching years behind me, I was amazed by the assortment of ways in which the factors were implemented and by the numerous other possibilities they suggest for updating existing free reading programs and developing new ones. In the next chapter, I will describe each factor in depth.

2

The Eight Factors for SSR Success

To begin with, I'll provide a short definition of each of the eight Factors for SSR Success and explain how they were included in the effective SSR programs that I reviewed. I selected only studies where students increased in reading comprehension or developed more positive attitudes toward reading. Later, in Chapter Five, I will suggest practical methods to help you plan what I call "stacked for success" SSR programs—those which contain all eight factors. We need to remember that these definitions emerged from the studies themselves and may easily be expanded to fit new SSR programs. The studies simply provided a starting point for identifying what components free reading programs should include to achieve maximum effectiveness.

Factor One: Access

One factor which all of the successful programs included was access to books. Access means that trade books, magazines, comics, newspapers, and other reading materials were provided directly to the students in a variety of ways instead of requiring the students to bring something from home to read. Many programs provided "book floods," or large numbers of reading materials within the classrooms where the students engaged in free reading. Depending upon the experiment, on the average as few as one-and-a-half and as many as eleven books per student were available in the classrooms. Though books were often purchased, sometimes city library books were checked out and then housed in the school classrooms for two to three weeks at a time. In order to get the greatest benefit from a beginning, smaller pool of books, frequently reading materials were systematically exchanged or rotated among students. In Fader's (1976) famous reform-school study, students were given two paperbacks at the beginning of the school year and allowed the practice of trading them in for others as they finished reading them. Book borrowing was scheduled twice a week for everyone, and current periodicals were added several times a week to English and social studies classes.

Aside from stocking books in the classroom libraries and centers, some programs enabled students to have access to books in other ways. Groups were offered opportunities to visit the school or city libraries or to order books from school book clubs at reduced prices. In one case, teachers actually helped children to apply for their own library cards, and then took students on a field trip to the city library (Kaminsky 1992). Where access to materials was still not sufficient through classroom and community library collections, students were helped to order selected books through inter-library loan systems. The key to providing access in all of these programs was that the researchers made sure that students were directly provided with a large number of readily available reading materials. The burden did not fall upon the readers to locate their own reading materials outside of school.

Factor Two: Appeal

A second factor, book appeal, was included in the successful programs approximately seventy-eight percent of the time. Broadly defined, appeal means that reading materials are sufficiently interesting and provocative enough for students to want to read them. A crucial element of book appeal is self-selection, or the opportunity for students to choose what they want to read regardless of the teacher's preferences (though always with "classroom appropriate" guidelines in mind). Almost all of the successful groups offered students opportunities to self-select their books for the SSR period. Self-selection is important because it is difficult for readers to develop a sense of ownership and purpose if someone else is telling them what to read.

Another component of book appeal includes offering a wide variety of sources, types, and genres of reading materials to suit students' interests, as well as an extensive range of readability levels so that all readers can find something they like and can handle independently. The goal is to be sure that everyone has access to materials that they not only want to read—but **can** read. Materials that will pique everyone's interests and offer a wide range of readability must be available so that the least proficient to the most proficient readers in the classroom can enthusiastically engage in free reading. A notable feature of the successful SSR programs is that special effort was put into including a wide spectrum of materials in order to make classroom collections genuinely inviting to students. Some researchers replaced conventional materials, such as traditional anthologies, with trade books and storybooks related to different content areas. In order to ensure that materials were comprehensible for ESL students, their appropriateness for students' ages, interests, and readability levels was taken into account before selection. Teachers in the studies also found that attractive materials that incorporated natural language, local themes, and an element of excitement or humor were especially appealing to students of all ages.

In addition to books, other more nonconventional materials were added to classroom bookshelves and bins. Some students were offered a mixture of magazines, newspapers, pamphlets, and comic books, sources not typically used in the regular classrooms. Materials with subject matter relevant to content area courses in the curriculum were used freely, and hardbound books were often replaced with paperbacks to make the materials more tempting.

Other methods of making books more enticing in some of the programs involved displaying materials attractively and letting students have a voice in the purchase and/or arrangement of new materials. Classrooms contained colorful book displays and wire book spinners for paperbacks, and teachers encouraged students to attach book jackets to bulletin boards to advertise popular titles.

Building on students' enthusiasm for reading was also a critical part of making books inviting in these studies. In some cases, students were consulted about the titles they wished to add to classroom collections. Where materials were funded by special grants, students were even occasionally allowed to keep particular books, thereby adding the additional allure of private ownership. In some classes, if students found materials they especially enjoyed, they could utilize class bulletin boards or Noticeboards, where they displayed book reviews, posters, cartoons, and crosswords inspired by their reading in order to urge other readers to sample the selections.

Because students will not read if they are uninspired by the materials provided; because they must read for their own purposes in order to sustain their motivation; and because they must have materials available that they *can* read when they decide to read, appeal is a crucial element of a free reading program. The kinds of materials available and the ways in which they are displayed play a large part in helping young people to find enticing books that will persuade them to want to keep reading.

Factor Three: Conducive Environment

Whenever we find something good to read, it is logical that we are drawn to comfortable, quiet places—surroundings where we won't be disturbed. In all of the successful free reading programs that I analyzed, a quiet, uninterrupted environment was provided. And, in some of them, special locations for reading were adopted and accoutrements added to make the atmosphere more personal and homey.

In reviewing the studies, I found that a large percentage of the successful programs utilized traditional classroom settings and simply built in the element of uninterrupted and silent reading time. Talking or discussion was discouraged, so even though students sat in their regular seats, they were protected from noise or interruptions when they read. Teachers in one group put "Do Not Disturb" signs on the classroom doors and ignored attempts at interruption by the students until the attempts finally subsided (Greaney 1970). Also, in some classes a bell timer was set so that students would not be distracted by having to keep track of the predicted ending time for the SSR period.

In some programs, though, researchers developed conducive environments by choosing neutral locations for free reading—ones unlike typical classroom settings. Students in one study were asked to meet at the researcher's place of work every day after school; away from an academic arena, they felt more relaxed and open to doing pleasure reading (Hafiz and Tudor 1985). In similar studies, children were allowed to read in Media Centers or Reading Centers, separate from the regular classrooms. In these locations they were told that they were not allowed to do any

Figure 2–1. Chris and Thu find their niche in a classroom corner.

kind of reading related to homework assignments (viewed as "school tasks"), only to read for pleasure.

Finally, some of the programs appealed to the students' need to be social. Because readers often feel more comfortable when they can interact with peers, researchers offered programs which included silent, uninterrupted reading for a specified period of time and then allowed students to talk about their books informally in a risk-free, low-anxiety context. In other programs, where students were not given time to interact after SSR, they were allowed to sit with friends during the reading period, adding to a sense of camaraderie and community spirit.

It was valuable to see that in most of the studies, comfort and quiet were the main criteria for achieving an effective reading environment. Somehow I had visualized a carpeted room with throw pillows and bean bag chairs as being a necessary part of a truly conducive setting. Certainly, rooms with homey furnishings may add to the appeal of the reading environment, but it is good to know that simply providing a pleasant, quiet place can do the trick just as well. When funds are not available to buy special accoutrements, a quiet, informal setting can go a long way toward supporting readers in their quest for an insulated environment in which to lose themselves temporarily in a good book.

Factor Four: Encouragement

There is no assurance that putting students in a conducive environment with a wide range of interesting books will actually stimulate them to read. Those who have already found reading to be exhilarating will jump at the chance, but those who have yet to be hooked on books won't recognize what a satisfying experience they're being offered. Without encouragement to read, reluctant readers may never see what devoted readers already know: that reading can open doors for them in ways that no other activity can, that it's pleasurable, and that it can become a rewarding, lifetime habit.

In the successful studies that I reviewed, ninety percent were provided with a specific form of encouragement to read. One way that students were encouraged was by the involvement of teachers with them in sharing and discussing books. Several of the programs offered readers the chance to have special time or individual conferences with their teacher after the reading period to discuss the materials that they had been reading. In one case, teachers read aloud to their classes after the free reading period, and then students shared ideas about the individual books that they had been reading independently, as well as about the class book that the teacher had read aloud. In most of the groups they were also asked to participate in activities designed to extend their book experiences with their teachers and classmates. These after-reading opportunities included various forms of interactive listening, speaking, and writing activities in order to promote the desire for further reading.

Another form of encouragement, which the majority of programs included, was adult modeling of reading while the students read. When teachers, administrators and classroom assistants read, they projected their conviction that reading was both pleasurable and worthwhile, disenfranchising students of the notion that reading in school was nothing more than a school task. Students came to see that the adults valued reading, and they, in turn, were willing to try it themselves.

Also, teachers and staff members in the studies sometimes acted as resource persons. One Media Center specialist made recommendations to match students' interests and helped these young people to find self-selected books from other sources when they were not available at the school site. In another study, a special "reading counselor" was provided with whom students could schedule book conferences up to twice a week at first—and then more often later, as requested.

Some researchers included an even broader range of adult support, which reached beyond a single classroom. In one group, parents were brought into the act in two specific ways: by becoming involved in the original development of the reading program, and then by working with their children at home. To enlist parent participation, the teacher mailed newsletters outlining program goals; asked parents to provide input for the program and purchase reading materials for their children; and suggested ideas to support at-home reading. In other groups, students received all-staff support; adults in every class tempted students to engage in the "privileged activity" of free reading, urging them to bring more books from home, buy them, exchange them, and find them in the library.

Finally, a social element of encouragement was introduced in some programs. After the reading period, students were asked to share "the good parts" with their friends. Researchers remarked upon the strong incentive of peer perspectives, noticing that when some students—particularly the class leaders—began to enjoy reading, their peers were given "a strong incentive to act accordingly" (Jenkins 1957, 501). As reading became viewed as an acceptable (and even pleasurable) activity, more classmates jumped on the bandwagon.

In various ways, then, the effective SSR programs included tangible forms of motivation to read and showed us that in order to engage students in the habitual act of reading for pleasure, it is important to secure the support of teachers, staff members, friends, and parents. After all, if our ultimate goal is to spur students on to become lifelong readers, any type of encouragement which leads to this end should be considered a viable part of SSR program planning.

Factor Five: Staff Training

When I speak with educators about offering SSR time to students, I get the impression that many in-school free reading programs are based on two premises: (1) that students should read in order to get better at reading and (2) that teachers simply need to carve out class time in order for them to do it. While I subscribe to the first idea, I am skeptical of the second one. When analyzing the successful studies, I noticed an emphasis on teacher training that more carefully clarified the teacher's role in a free reading program. As we will see, it is distinctly active, rather than passive; and it goes far beyond the obvious requirement of providing quiet time to read in school. In fact, I believe that the reason this factor was not as consistently incorporated into the successful programs as some of the other factors were is because many people—even well-intentioned educators—believe in the premise that to "do SSR" is a simple matter that requires little planning.

Approximately forty percent of the studies incorporated some type of teacher training into their free reading programs. In these studies, researchers provided specific staff development activities to help teachers establish practical guidelines for implementation and develop their roles as active facilitators in helping students to connect with books. In most cases, the training was done at the school sites where the programs took place. The workshop presenters or coordinators gave demonstration lessons and sometimes provided sets of notes outlining SSR methodology—which typically tended to be modeled on the early McCracken (1971) guidelines. Some advisors also visited schools to give brief demonstration lessons and practice sessions for their teachers. In one program, teachers were given tape-slide presentations, supplemented by printed SSR guidelines. In another, they were asked to read the literature on SSR and study what had been written about the philosophy and implementation of self-selected reading programs. Based on what they learned, these teachers then purchased a large collection of materials with a wide range of difficulty levels and developed ways to introduce the program to students and parents at their school.

The fact that some researchers in the successful programs made it a point to train teachers in the art of free reading may at first seem surprising, especially when we consider that the type of training they provided was actually quite varied. What seems to be critical is that they focused on motivating teachers to learn strategies for linking students with books, highlighting the importance of having all of the participating adults "buy into" the concept of free reading. Because they were given a good deal of support and the opportunity to work together to develop their programs, teachers were committed, feeling that they had a major investment in the success of the students. The effectiveness of these programs illustrates that educators who develop free reading programs must truly understand and believe in the philosophy underlying them. We cannot merely stand back and tell our students that reading is good for them but instead must be willing to take the necessary time to help them make matches with reading materials that they will savor.

Factor Six: Non-Accountability

In the original McCracken approach to SSR, one of the guidelines was that no reports or records were kept. The idea that students should be able to read freely without an emphasis on assessment of comprehension or reading growth was carried through in eighty-seven percent of the successful programs.

In some of the groups, a focus on non-accountability was made clear by omission of information; in the program descriptions, no mention was made of any activities that would qualify as monitoring or checking the students on what they had read. However, some of the researchers specifically discussed the lack of accountability in their programs and pinpointed the idea of providing non-evaluative atmospheres within which there were no requirements related to productive tasks or follow-up language work. Some groups omitted book reports or written exercises so that the children could read for enjoyment and practice, and others excluded all textbooks from the reading choices during SSR in order to focus on the pleasure-oriented aspect of reading.

Many of the researchers mentioned not allowing students to keep any kinds of records or reports because these activities seemed too much like school tasks and did not emphasize enough the pleasurable aspect of reading. In general, students were not asked to keep track of their reading materials, the book titles, or the numbers of pages read; and the teachers did not test students on the content. One researcher also asked students to put books down when they were not interesting enough and to select new ones—an authentic practice that most adults engage in when we are bored with our own reading choices.

The key to non-accountability, as indicated by these successful groups, is to omit any activity that gives students the message that they are responsible for completing a task, comprehending a particular portion of their reading, or showing they have made improvement in some way. In order to get the most enjoyment possible from their reading, they should feel no obligation associated with it. As habitual readers are well aware, the very knowledge that they have to do something with reading other than what they choose to do takes away from its magic. It keeps them from experiencing the enjoyment of just relaxing with a good book, which is the goal of an effective SSR program.

However, we can identify many activities that students do enjoy engaging in after they've read exciting books. They are very often social in nature and provide outlets for readers to share their enthusiasm with others. They are different from accountability measures and can be labeled, simply, as follow-up activities.

Factor Seven: Follow-up Activities

Follow-up activities encourage students to sustain their excitement about the books they have read. They are typically interactive in nature and offer opportunities for readers to channel their enthusiasm in creative and thoughtful ways. Of course, they may not include any components that readers may view as accountability measures; otherwise, their power is severely diminished.

Approximately fifty-three percent of the successful groups in the studies included some type of follow-up offerings to their students. By surveying the descriptions of the SSR programs, I found that many researchers did not view these activities as officially part of SSR—and I question whether perhaps some follow-up activities may actually have been incorporated into the programs but were not discussed because they were considered superfluous. Those that were described, however, often included the use of art, music, or science within performance-based contexts. One group engaged in role playing, as well as doing art work and writing. Significantly, the origin of the activities was always determined by the story, and new learning took place at the point of interest. Other groups drew and wrote about story themes, constructed group murals related to their books, made their own books, and performed as actors and mimes. Some students also participated in the Language Experience Approach, a method by which they dictated their own stories to the teacher, who wrote them down for the students to read as a new text. In this way, readers became authors and then readers again, emphasizing the interrelated nature of the reading and writing process. In other programs, students participated in oral reading, puppetry, dramatizations, and science experiments, which resulted from ideas gleaned from students' reading.

A few groups eliminated the idea of projects and products entirely and simply allowed students to discuss what they had read. Readers became involved in teacher-to-student, student-to-student, and whole-class discussions. In one case, students bonded with peers who had chosen the same book and discussed it in small group settings, a practice similar to the use of literacy circles; then they made drawings of the major incidents in their books, which they elaborated upon further. Other programs offered weekly thirty-minute book-sharing and question/answer periods involving the entire class.

Some researchers took a more creative approach to book sharing and offered imaginative ways for students to interest others in the books they had read. In one case, students read passages, poems, and funny stories aloud to their classmates in

Figure 2–2. Two high school juniors prepare to do Book Talks after SSR.

an effort to encourage them to do further reading. Another researcher took a "hard sell" approach: In addition to having students engage in peer read-alouds and other sharing activities, she embellished her follow-up program with "media-like" activities. Students designed their own book covers to "sell" book choices to others, and they read story-based fictionalized current events to their classmates as they adopted news-anchor personas, using microphones (Kaminsky 1992).

It is easy to see how these kinds of activities can motivate students to want to become involved with books—and then to want to pursue reading further. The SSR studies highlight the wide variety of approaches that we can take when providing follow-up experiences for students—but of course, they represent only a beginning. The array of possibilities is extensive and very exciting. The only caution we must observe is that we do not ask students to do anything that seems evaluative in nature. Otherwise, we make the mistake of crossing over the line which divides follow-up experiences from accountability measures.

Factor Eight: Distributed Time to Read

It is obvious that students need time to read in free reading programs, so when I started to look at the successful studies, the real question I was trying to answer was how much time they should be given and how often they should be given it. Knowing how schools and programs differ, I frankly expected to see large ranges in the amounts of time offered during each SSR period. In general, though, readers were given between fifteen and thirty minutes to read, with the exception of a few groups, which were offered longer sessions periodically.

In fact, it wasn't the range of time that varied so much as the frequency with which the free reading time was provided. In ninety-seven percent of the successful programs, the researchers offered free reading time to the students at least twice a week. This frequency pattern became the yardstick for what I called the "distributed time" programs. And, more than half of these programs offered SSR on a daily basis. Interestingly, when looking at some of the less successful programs in the studies, I noticed that students were sometimes given time to read for longer stretches of time, but on a monthly, bi-monthly, weekly, or bi-weekly basis, so I characterized these cases as "massed time to read"—or "all at once" programs. Though it is laudable that students were given some time to read in school, they didn't do it often enough to make it habit-forming, and making reading an habitual activity appeared to be a characteristic that differentiated the successful programs from the unsuccessful ones.

Several of the researchers pointed out that getting students to read on a regular basis was the key to their development as readers. Since students don't always have opportunities to read at home, they must be provided time to read in school. It follows, then, that time to read must also be offered on a regular basis in order to promote the habit of reading.

Implications for Teaching

Having seen how the successful programs in these studies incorporated the eight factors I have just discussed, the logical and necessary question for us to ask is what the implications are for developing effective programs ourselves. My view is that we can learn by looking at what works well and taking similar approaches. If our goal is the same as the goal of these programs—to help students become better readers and to enjoy reading more—then it follows that we can start by using these programs as models and taking the best from them. In Chapter 3 I will discuss an attempt that a colleague and I made to do exactly that.

3

Piloting a "Stacked for Success" Program

At the time that I was reading literature on the eight factors, I was teaching high school ESL students who were enrolled in classes called Developmental Reading. My school was in a Los Angeles County urban area, and our students came from a wide variety of language groups, with Armenian, Spanish, and Korean being the largest. I had previously been offering my students free reading time during each class period; but with the new information gathered from the analysis of the successful SSR programs, I found that I had violated some of the eight factors without even realizing it.

I was determined to incorporate the eight factors into the SSR program for my five classes and see what results I might achieve. Like other teachers who had told me about their SSR attempts, I had often noticed that some students were never completely engaged. Often, they became distracted, complained about not being able to find good books, and constantly asked when the reading time would be over. Not infrequently, these same students tried to disturb others who wanted to read. Though I managed to keep the free reading sessions going for the sake of those who appreciated and benefited from them, it was sometimes a struggle.

After identifying the eight Factors for SSR Success, I felt more prepared to handle some of the problematic issues of implementation. In fact, I could already target some of my mistakes, recognizing that the factors of access to books, book appeal, and encouragement were particularly weak in my classes. I wanted to restructure the existing program into one that was "stacked for success"—that is, one that included all eight factors. However, my ultimate goal was not only to see what might happen with my own students, but to learn lessons that would benefit other teachers, too. First, I needed to develop a strong rationale for offering SSR programs to high school students—and to show how they would benefit not only native English speakers, but ESL students, as well.

Benefits of Free Reading for Secondary Students

Few people would question that children who are beginning to read should become involved with books. In fact, much has been written about creative ways to help them do this. Approaches such as guided reading (reading instruction in which the teacher provides the structure and purpose for reading and for responding to the material read) and shared reading, (a technique whereby the teacher involves a group of children in the reading of a particular Big Book in order to help them learn aspects of beginning literacy and develop reading strategies), plus a wide array of other interactive methods are available to elementary school teachers for engaging children in the reading process.

If students are to become fully proficient readers, however, they eventually need to break away from the scaffolding activities that support them in their roles as emergent readers and begin to read some materials independently. This change is not something that happens at once. Instead, it occurs gradually. For students to become independent readers, they require opportunities to spend time with books on their own, aside from the interactive reading activities that they do with their classmates and the teacher. In first or second grade, they may begin by simply looking at the pictures or turning pages and telling themselves a story they have heard someone read aloud to them. Some children also begin to decode printed text, if highly predictable, interesting, and comprehensible materials are accessible to them. Once children are able to enjoy free reading time—and to see themselves as "readers," the transition from emergent reader to proficient reader accelerates quickly.

An adult who walked into an elementary class and saw children engaged in free reading would probably smile and nod, pleased that the school was doing its job. But this is not always how the public views the secondary scene. Some critics believe that SSR has no place in the upper-grade curriculum. In fact, if we were to poll the general population, we would probably find that most people are surprised to hear that middle school, junior high, and high school students would benefit from free reading. The assumption is that by the end of elementary school, children know how to read and do not need time in school to do it. Many people would even say that free reading takes away from valuable time spent on core curriculum. This perspective is similar to the view of a parent described by Jim Trelease (1995) in *The Read Aloud Handbook:* "He's in the top fourth grade reading group—why should I read to him? Isn't that why we're sending him to school, so he'll learn to read by himself?" (45–46). Trelease's position is that reading aloud motivates students to become interested in books and to want to be able to read higher-level materials, just as adults do. He maintains that it is a practice that builds readers' listening vocabularies—the reservoirs from which reading vocabularies come. Most important, he stresses that it should be fostered throughout the school years, even into the upper grades.

So it is with free reading. In their book, *The Case for Late Intervention: Once a Good Reader, Always a Good Reader*, Krashen and McQuillan (1996) argue that although not all students are avid readers by the time they reach secondary school, it is never too late to hook them on the one habit that will make them truly proficient and lifelong lovers of reading: reading. If students aren't reading at home—and there are many reasons why they aren't—they can and should be reading at school.

A good deal has been written about the special needs of young adults. They are torn by the demands of school, home, friends, outside jobs, extracurricular activities, and numerous other pressures. In fact, it has been reported that certain kinds of leisure activities remain consistently popular with teenagers. In particular, as we have learned from the earliest attempts to record youth leisure activities to the most recent adolescent research, socializing with friends and participating in sports remain the favorite pursuits of adolescents (Moffitt and Wartella 1992). It is no wonder that reading for pleasure is often the activity that rates as least important on their list of priorities. Actually, there is a negative correlation between grade level and free voluntary reading: the higher the grade level that students are in, the less often they read for pleasure (Wiscont 1990).

Aside from the temptations of other activities, another reason why the reading habit does not always develop is that when readers reach the upper levels of schooling, they may find a split between what they are asked to read in school and what they enjoy reading. This can set up what Carlsen and Sherrill (1988) term "an adversarial relationship between the young persons and the school and may even result in the students feeling a sense of inadequacy about their own reading tastes" (20). Many teachers insist that high school students read what is considered to be "good" literature, often the classics, leaving students no other options that might spark their interest to pursue further reading. Yet we know that "light reading" can be a powerful conduit to more difficult reading (Cho and Krashen 1994, Russikoff and Pilgreen 1994). It is important that students have opportunities to set personal purposes for reading, which can guide their selections. Though schools require students to read specific assigned texts and course-related materials to match specified curricula, a sustained silent reading period can offer the kind of "reading for fun" situation that is missing from young people's school days.

Certainly, one potent influence on adolescents' reading habits is their peer group. Prompted by the need to keep up socially with a particular friend or group of peers, teens often make their choices according to their group's perspective. Gallo (1968) highlights this particularly powerful form of peer pressure in his survey of grade eleven, remarking that "what students have to say to each other about the books they read has far more influence on future reading than any other person or any other device" (536). If adolescents feel dependent upon group choices, they will not seek out reading choices that match their own interests or needs. If their peer group does not view reading as an acceptable activity, they will not read at all.

It is our goal, then, to make reading acceptable. We must find ways to help students make matches with books that will engage and excite them. As teenagers find reading materials that speak to their own needs and interests, they become willing to share with their friends. The first wave of peer acceptance can generate other waves, encouraging the cycle to continue. Eventually, students may become less dependent upon others' opinions and secure enough to pursue new reading interests on their own.

Once students start to read, they typically develop interests in particular subject areas or genres. Adults can then direct them to books that provide more in-

Figure 3–1. Marieta and Miganoush share a possible book selection before SSR.

formation or experience in these categories. Sometimes students will be intrigued by the work of a popular author, and, given the guidance to find the books written by that author and the opportunity to read them, will voraciously devour everything by that writer. Other students, having previously been instructed to read only "good literature," will finally discover a stimulating genre they have not encountered before. Impelled by the privilege of self-selecting books of interest, they will read everything available in that particular category. I vividly recall one tenth grade ESL student in my Developmental Reading class who told me that she had never read a whole book in her entire life. When she discovered the *Sweet Valley Twins* series, written at a level she could understand, she began checking out book after book. Another boy with a similar reading history discovered S. E. Hinton and promptly read *The Outsiders* and *That Was Then, This Is Now*—then asked to go to the school library for more titles. When he had exhausted everything Hinton had written, he asked me if I had any information about the author! The next day I handed him a copy of her biography, to keep. What we learn from such students is that when they are given a supportive, nonthreatening environment and access to appealing reading materials, they can very quickly be transformed from non-readers into bookworms.

Books can also offer teenagers a way to identify with characters who have experiences in common with them. Reed (1988) acknowledges that early adolescence is often a lonely and frustrating time for young adults attempting to establish a personal identify, as well as to develop relationships with their peers. She identifies Young Adult (YA) books as a source of reading that can make them feel less alone, while encouraging them to pursue more mature reading interests. Authors of YA books can help teenagers deal with difficult times in life because they "become anonymous mentors who are able to speak to early adolescents as no adult on the scene can" (22). I know this is true because a student of mine whose mother had a drinking problem became motivated to read *Please Don't Ask Me to Love You* by Ann Schraff. She was able to see similarities between her own situation and the protagonist's—and was absolutely unable to put the book down, even when SSR time was over. I'm convinced that she had never read a book so quickly in her whole life.

My daughter, too, found an author she adored and who "spoke to her" when she was fourteen. She began reading Lurlene McDaniels' novels, in which teenagers and their families have to face life-threatening illnesses. When a long-time friend of hers became gravely ill, she shared with me that she felt better prepared to deal with the situation because she had read the McDaniels book about a young girl with cystic fibrosis, the same illness her friend had. I became aware of just how important it is for teachers to have substantial backgrounds in Young Adult literature so that we can make recommendations to suit our students' tastes and needs. As

Nancy, a middle school teacher in Pomona, put it, "We can't hook them on books unless we give them the right bait!" I couldn't agree more.

Appropriateness of Free Reading for Nonnative Speakers of English

Given solid evidence to support the development of free reading programs in the secondary grades, we must also ask where our ESL students—those who are acquiring English as a subsequent language—fit into the picture. After all, the materials they read in school are primarily in English. My high school ESL students, for example, could read and write in their primary languages, but their reading levels in English ranged from approximately second to sixth grade. I needed to determine what specific benefits free reading would offer them.

Mangubhai and Elley (1982) have focused on the issue of free reading for ESL students, pointing out that "while reading is widely encouraged in first-language acquisition for a variety of reasons, its role has been repeatedly played down in ESL" (151). They believe this is because reading is seldom regarded as a means of extending children's grasp of the language. Exposure to unfamiliar words and structures is thought to confuse the learners, to cause errors in interpretation, and to distort the pronunciation of new words. They suggest instead that reading has a positive, constructive role to play in second-language acquisition. Unlike the oral-first approach, which restricts language growth, extensive reading allows students to progress naturally and quickly.

Similarly, Krashen (1987) tells us that non-native speakers of English can acquire it in only one way—by understanding messages or by receiving "comprehensible imput" in a low-anxiety environment. This is, he argues, precisely what free reading provides. Teachers can ensure that large amounts of interesting, comprehensible reading materials are available so that when students are engaged in free reading, they are more easily able to concentrate on the message without being focused primarily on the code.

Also, when ESL students read for pleasure, they develop the competence they need to move from the beginning "ordinary conversational" levels to higher levels of literacy. So, for all of its virtues, the Natural Approach that is used in beginning ESL instruction has its limits. Students are not able to use their second language for more demanding purposes such as reading the classics, engaging in the serious study of literature, using the language for international business, or for advanced scholarship. As Krashen (1993) notes, free reading is one way of extending the principles underlying the Natural Approach to the intermediate level; it can help to bridge the gap between easier and more difficult reading materials. By combining free reading with the usual kinds of assigned reading in a literature-based language arts class, we can offer students the perfect opportunity to develop second-language literacy.

Another benefit of free reading is that the type of input that is received by doing it is qualitatively different from what a non-native English acquirer receives through usual daily contact with the language. This is true because students can explore a wider range of topics and situations, with the accompanying linguistic elements, than they would encounter in their everyday oral interactions. Not surprisingly, in a project designed to investigate the language acquisition background of students in the Intensive English Program in Hong Kong, researchers Gradman and Hanania (1992) found that the one background factor that had the strongest relationship with level of proficiency was outside reading—the extent to which students had read outside class, for information or pleasure.

In addition to providing opportunities for ESL students to read better, free reading is also a facilitator of overall language development. In a two-year study on Fijian primary schools, by the end of the first year, the free reading group had made substantial improvement in the receptive skills of reading and listening. By the end of the second year, however, this improvement had extended to all aspects of the subjects' English language abilities, including oral and written production, leading the researchers to call this spread of effect a "most striking finding" (Elley and Mangubhai 1983, 404). Tse and McQuillan (1998) reached similar conclusions at the end of their study of second-language students who did extensive reading and received no grammar instruction during a ten-week session. The majority of the students found reading to be superior to traditional instruction "not only in terms of pleasure but also in perceived benefits in language acquisition" (266).

Finally, free reading has the potential to change ESL students' conceptions about the reading process as a whole. As Cho and Krashen (1994) have found, many students do not believe that reading will help them. They believe that they will best be served by learning rules and practicing often, with lots of corrective feedback; and they view reading as hard work, which entails word-by-word decoding of difficult texts. Also, it is sometimes difficult to find the texts that are both interesting and readable. Effective free reading programs can expose students to a variety of light reading options that satisfy their desire for material that is both enjoyable and comprehensible, and they can help non-native English language acquirers come to view reading as a pleasant activity, rather than a task, that will lead to language acquisition.

The Pilot SSR Study

Armed with information that supported the development of free reading programs for high school native English speakers and ESL students, I was ready to start the planning and implementation of a new free reading program with my own five classes of students. I made arrangements to collect data and to carry out the necessary statistical analyses with Barry Gribbons, a colleague of mine at the University of Southern California, whose specialty was educational evaluation. We shared the goal of documenting the specific effects of an SSR program that included all eight factors.

Our immediate objective was to see what tangible results the students in such a program in my own classes could achieve in one semester. Our long-range goal was to share these results so that other teachers might become interested and join the SSR effort in their own schools. To accomplish both goals, we decided to run a pilot program with five sections of my high school ESL students. Because the pilot program was designed to contain all eight of the identified factors, we considered it to be "stacked for success." To us, this meant that it had the greatest potential for effectiveness.

Inclusion of the Eight Factors

Access To gather a wide variety of reading materials for our classroom library, I appealed to the principal of my school for financial assistance to purchase books and fund magazine subscriptions, which all five classes of students could use. Concerned about declining test scores in reading and enthusiastic about encouraging students to read more, he approved a purchase order for $850.00, which paid for about 250 books to supplement the 250 that were already in the classroom.

Appeal We already had a variety of materials in the classroom, including books written in languages other than English. However, I gave my students an interest inventory to see what kinds of materials they wanted to add to the classroom collection. They mainly selected magazines, comic books, and series books, so I subscribed, bought, and borrowed to match their requests.

Conducive Environment To create an appropriate environment, I added READ posters to the walls—the kind where celebrities and pop artists are featured, advocating the importance of reading. I also asked one of my students, who is a gifted artist, to make a sign to hang outside my door during SSR: "Please Do Not Disturb! We're Reading!" The classroom contained circular tables, which could seat four students each, and the chairs were comfortable. Whenever we received phone calls, I politely asked the callers to try again after SSR. As time passed, the students began to refer to their SSR time as their "bubble time," the few minutes each day when they could relax in a safe, enclosed atmosphere where no one could enter. They became irate when a fire drill or announcement over the PA system dared to burst the bubble.

Encouragement To offer encouragement to read, I did a variety of activities. I shared with my students what the research said about the effectiveness of SSR programs. I explained that their reading ability, as well as their spelling, grammar, vocabulary, and writing, would improve if they read more. I told them tales of how I used to travel across the United States with my parents in the summertime, arguing with my brother over who would first get to read the best and newest comic books during those endless hours in the car. I even admitted that I used to read with my flashlight under the covers at night, long after my parents had insisted that I go to sleep. I explicitly told them that they *should* read—that they would discover a whole new exciting world waiting for them. And, *I* read when *they* read during SSR.

Distributed Time to Read Students were provided with approximately twelve minutes of time each day to read whatever they liked. A timer was set, and the reading began!

Non-Accountability There were no book reports, mandated journal entries, or comprehension checks. I must admit that the students were skeptical at first. In fact, they asked me what the "catch" was. After all, constant evaluation by teachers was part of their usual school experience, or schemata. As time passed, however,

Figure 3–2. Class tablemates discuss interesting book highlights.

they came to expect and appreciate that no one would violate their personal reading domains with questions or assignments.

Follow-up Activities Students shared information about their books if they decided they wanted to. Twice a week students were given five minutes after SSR time to tell peers about the most exciting parts of their books. These activities were not sophisticated, but they gave readers a way to extend their enthusiasm and to promote even more interest in reading among their classmates. Often, students would sign up on waiting lists for particular books after these sharing sessions.

Staff Training As for the staff training factor, I considered myself as well-versed in SSR implementation as I could initially be after spending so much time investigating the thirty-two studies, but I also knew that I would learn more as the program progressed (which I did, tremendously!).

Goals and Results of the Pilot Study

We started with five basic goals, all of which dealt with comprehension and motivation to read, two areas which the literature on Sustained Silent Reading had shown could be developed substantially through free voluntary reading. The pilot study objectives included the following:

1. improved reading comprehension
2. greater enjoyment of reading
3. more frequent engagement in outside(home) pleasure reading
4. belief in self as a better reader
5. utilization of a wider range of sources for pleasure reading

In order to answer these questions, we developed an informal Pilot Student Questionnaire (see Appendix D), and used it in conjunction with the Stanford Diagnostic Reading Test. In September, we administered the pretest version of the Student Questionnaire and the pretest form of the SDRT to my 125 intermediate-level high school ESL students who represented approximately thirty different primary-language groups—with Armenian, Spanish and Korean being predominant. Then, the students participated in a "stacked for success" SSR program that ran for sixteen weeks. In January, we administered the posttest version of the Student Questionnaire and the posttest form of the SDRT.

We were thrilled to discover that all five goals were met, which was a more remarkable finding than we anticipated, given the short-term nature of the program. The results included the following:

Improved Reading Comprehension Students improved an average of 9 raw score points from the pretest to the posttest on the Stanford Diagnostic Reading Test.

This gain translated into 15 months of growth in reading comprehension in only 16 weeks, from an average reading level of 3.7 to 5.3—almost a year and a half's progress in one semester. (See Appendix E, Table 1.)

Greater Enjoyment of Reading Students clearly liked pleasure reading more after the four-month program, as indicated by the Pilot Student Questionnaire. While more than 26 percent of the students reported that they liked it just "a little" at the beginning, only 4 percent reported that they liked it a "little" at the end; while 26 percent reported that they liked it "a lot" at the beginning, more than 46 percent liked it "a lot" at the end. (See Appendix E, Table 2.)

More Frequent Engagement in Outside (Home) Pleasure Reading Students more frequently engaged in outside pleasure reading at the end of the program, as indicated by the Pilot Student Questionnaire. While 8 percent of the students reported that they "never" did outside pleasure reading before the program started, fewer than 1 percent reported that they "never" engaged in outside pleasure reading at the end; while 20 percent reported that they engaged in outside pleasure reading "often" before the program started, more than 40 percent reported that they engaged in it "often" by the end of the program. (See Appendix E, Table 3.)

Belief in Self as a Better Reader At the end of the program, almost all of the students believed that they had improved in reading, as indicated by the Pilot Student Questionnaire. Fewer than 2 percent of the students reported that they did not perceive themselves to be better readers than they were at the beginning of the program, while more than 36 percent felt they had improved "some," and 62 percent felt they had improved "a lot." (See Appendix E, Table 4.)

Utilization of a Wider Range of Sources for Pleasure Reading At the end of the program, results of the Pilot Student Questionnaire indicated that students were less dependent on the use of classroom library collections than they were at the beginning. Use of school library materials doubled; use of books brought from home doubled; use of books borrowed from friends tripled; and use of books from a bookstore or book club almost quadrupled. (See Appendix E, Table 5.)

Implications of the Pilot Study

The results of the study were quite favorable, leading us to conclude that in-school free reading programs have the potential to help high school ESL students develop more positive attitudes toward reading and increase their reading comprehension. However, though it was tempting to suspect that the SSR program was responsible for this group's trend toward improvement, we could not show a causal link between the SSR program and the improvement. Since there was no comparison group in the study (another school without such an SSR program), we could be not be certain that the growth we saw was a result of the SSR program itself and not a result of other variables.

Excited about the trends we saw in the pilot study, though, we decided to devote the time and energy it would take to do a valid research study in which one group would be given an SSR program containing all eight factors—and a second group would be given an SSR program with fewer factors. Of course, our hypothesis was that the "stacked for success" program would be more effective.

4

Design and Description of the Formal Study

Setting Up the Study

To set up a study with a credible research design, we needed to identify an experimental group that would have a "stacked for success" SSR program containing all eight factors and a control group that would have an SSR program containing fewer factors. The experimental group was composed of a new sample of my own students, while the comparison group included students from another high school in the same district. The two groups were comparable in terms of their language backgrounds, socioeconomic status, ages, grade levels, and gender proportions. Only intermediate level ESL students in grades 10–12 were included. For the purposes of the study, my school became known as the Home School, and the other high school became known as the Community School. One hundred thirty-one students in the Home School and 117 students in the Community School participated.

Staff members from both schools had been invited to attend a fall district staff-development workshop on language acquisition and free voluntary reading, presented by Stephen Krashen. Although this event was not originally designed as part of the formal research study we had planned, it served as a motivating factor in urging the Community School to develop its own SSR program, which until then, had not been operating on a full-scale basis in their ESL classes. Some teachers had provided SSR opportunities for their students, while others had not.

The presentation was timely because district test scores in reading had recently been the subject of discussion, and the administrators who attended became enthusiastic about supporting their teachers in developing SSR programs. As a result, special funding was made available at both school sites for the creation of classroom libraries and supplementation of school library holdings.

The basis for comparing the two schools was to gauge the effectiveness of the Home School's SSR program versus the Community School's SSR program. The real question was whether a "stacked for success" SSR program—that is, one with all eight factors—would be more successful than a minimally "stacked for success" SSR program—one with only some of the factors. However, until we actually observed the Community School's program, we could not be certain what those factors would be. Since we had not shared the results of our earlier Pilot Study (and the Factors for SSR Success) with the staff members there, we assumed the program probably would not include all eight of the components.

As planned, the Home School group participated in a "stacked for success" SSR program, one which contained all eight of the factors. However, after observation of the Community school, we determined that it participated in a minimally "stacked for success" SSR program, one which included four factors adequately, three factors partially, and one factor not at all.

Factors Implemented in the Home School Program

Access

Access to books was provided by purchasing new books to replace lost ones during the Pilot Study, which resulted in a total class library of more than 500 materials. Students could select books, magazines, newspapers, and comics from any other sources they wished, including the classroom collection, the school library, the public library, their homes, bookstores, and book clubs. Free class points earned from book club orders were used to buy additional books that the students wanted, as well. When students in our classes told older brothers and sisters about our class library, some of them, especially those who were Home School alumni, donated books that they had read and wanted to share with the school. We also subscribed to six different magazines which arrived on a weekly or monthly basis. Students signed up on waiting lists for titles that they especially enjoyed.

Appeal

Book appeal was incorporated by surveying students about their reading interests before the new books were purchased (see Appendix F for an example of the Interest Inventory). Also, my instructional aides and I assisted students in locating books by favorite authors or on special topics as the semester progressed. We had purposefully held back some of the money that our principal had appropriated for the classroom library. So, as our students became interested in specific series books or genres, we purchased additional materials, adding a measure of "personalized" attention and maintaining interest levels. My instructional assistants were particularly helpful in seeking out books or titles in which students expressed interest. Fortunately, the school librarian also worked closely with my classes to find materials that the students requested, and we sent students to meet with her and check out books on a regular basis. Of course, all reading materials were self-selected, and students were allowed to discontinue reading anything they did not enjoy in favor of something more interesting. We found that paperbacks were unquestionably more popular than hardback books, even when the titles were exactly the same.

Conducive Environment

We provided a physically comfortable area for reading. Students typically sat at round tables (with space for four students) in a carpeted and air-conditioned room. The rules for quiet and uninterrupted time were observed; no phone calls were taken, no office messengers were allowed to come in, and the "Please do not disturb" sign was hung on the outside of the classroom door. "READ" Posters, purchased from the American Library Association, were mounted on the walls, featuring popular movie stars and song artists. Our students even had a part in selecting the posters from the catalogue, and we rotated new ones in and old ones out during each quarter of the school year. After several weeks of settling down to the SSR routine, readers actually became irritated when announcements were made over the public address system or a fire or earthquake drill was initiated by the administration.

Encouragement

Encouragement to read was offered in a variety of ways: by informing students of the many ways in which free reading would support their literacy development in the areas of reading, spelling, vocabulary, grammar, and writing; by pointedly asking them to read when they were not fully engaged in reading; by adult modeling of the reading process as the students read; and by helping to link students with interesting books when they could not initially get "hooked." At the end of each class period, my aides and I would ask students if they had their free reading books checked out to take home for each evening, and each Friday we encouraged them to be sure they had interesting materials to read for the weekend. On Mondays, we collected their "Outside Pleasure Reading" sheets, which chronicled what they had read for pleasure the entire week before—and taped them to the walls so that others might see what they were reading and become interested in some of the same titles. (See Appendix G for an example of the Outside Pleasure Reading sheet.)

At the time that we began our SSR program, many of the students were also taking health and guidance classes in our high school. They were learning about the typical adolescent topics that are covered in such courses, including the risks

Figure 4–1. Keith checks out a book from the classroom library to take home for the evening.

of disease associated with indiscriminate dating practices. I often teased them on Friday afternoons by telling them to take a book home for the weekend, recommending it as a SAFE DATE. Of course, only I knew that the acronym represented the eight Factors for SSR Success: (S) staff training, (A) access, (F) follow-up activities, (E) encouragement, (D) direct access, (A) accountability (NON), (T) time to read, and (E) environment! It was my joke to remind them regularly that "a book makes a safe date" and their job to denigrate the idea in front of their peers. After all, what "cool" teen would admit to reading on weekends? But I know that some of them actually did read on Friday and Saturday nights because I saw their Outside Pleasure Reading sheets on Mondays—and chuckled to myself.

Staff Training

For me, staff training occurred as a combination of the following: reading the literature and descriptions of the effective SSR studies, analyzing the results of the Pilot Study, and attending Steve Krashen's presentation. I had been immersed in SSR philosophy, and I shared it continuously with my adult aides and the teachers in the rooms around me. In fact, other teachers at our school became intrigued by what the students were telling them about how much "fun" SSR was, and many of them began to implement free reading time in their classes, too. The principal of our school was willing to provide any teacher who wanted to begin doing SSR with a $500 start-up fund. It was truly inspiring when the art teacher invested in a wide range of beautifully illustrated art books about artists and styles; a social-studies teacher bought more than fifty different biographies of famous Americans, and the Spanish teacher purchased an entire series of *Sweet Valley High* books written in Spanish. During snack time, lunches, and faculty meetings, we would share stories about students who had never shown an interest in reading before but who were polishing off book after book during their free reading time in various classes. The camaraderie that developed among the teachers and students was strong, and I am certain that I stayed continuously motivated primarily because of the support of my colleagues and the responsiveness of our students.

Non-Accountability

There were no accountability measures of any kind following the SSR period, although some students voluntarily wrote personal responses on a reading record. (See Appendix H for an example of the Reading Record.) This record allowed them to keep track of the books and pages they were reading so that they could easily locate their new starting places each time they picked up their books again to read. It also provided a way for them to note their own responses to what they were reading. Often, some of these reflections would later become part of other kinds of writing assignments that they chose to do, such as the creation of poems, cartoon strips, and plays. Actually, I began by giving students cloze sentences, printed on the backs of the Reading Records, which they could complete with their own ideas and opinions (e.g., This story is exciting now because . . .). Later, students asked if they could add their own suggestions for responses, and we modified and added to the list we had started with. Eventually, it contained a majority of student responses, rather than teacher-created ones, which contributed to our students' sense of ownership in the reading-response process. (See Appendix I for an example of the Reading Responses sheet). Also, students took a great deal of pride in completing an entire Reading Record, which included ten school days of in-class reading. Somehow, it became a tangible form of closure, especially for students who had not previously read much. They could see what they had read, how much they had read, and what they had felt about their reading. Most important, it provided a method to help them realize that they could view themselves legitimately as members of the Literacy Club (Smith 1988b).

Follow-up Activities

Follow-up activities were developed on a weekly or bi-weekly basis: Students were allowed to read their reading responses or orally share exciting parts of their books with tablemates after the SSR time, and sign-up sheets were circulated so that students could get onto waiting lists for the more popular books. Once a month, on Fridays, I offered students the chance to create a book cover representing one of the more exciting or interesting books they had read during SSR. It may sound naive to expect that butcher paper, scissors, and colored markers would encourage high school students to participate in this project—but I cannot express how fully involved they became and how sophisticated some of the projects were. We put them on the bulletin boards and anywhere else they could be taped. Then, students volunteered to tell the class about the book covers and provide just enough information about the books to interest their peers without giving away the endings of the stories. The intensity of these sharing sessions always led to a new waiting list of classmates for any given title. These experiences were, in a word, thrilling.

Distributed Time to Read

Time to read silently was offered daily for approximately twelve to fifteen minutes, representing a "distributed" approach. We began each class period with SSR. As students entered the classroom, they either selected or brought the materials they wanted to read for the day. When the tardy bell rang, every student knew to be seated and ready to read. I typically sat in the seat of an absent student so that I would be in the midst of my students, rather than on the outskirts of the classroom. We read every day of the week unless there was a scheduled assembly or a fire or earthquake drill. Whenever an unusual event threatened to steal our time, inevitably students pretended to be "saved by the bell" from having to read. But I know that most of them were secretly disappointed because many of these same students often asked if they could have extra time for SSR the next day.

Factors Implemented in the Community School Program

A couple of weeks after the school year began, I was able to observe classrooms and to interview teachers from the Community School to find out how many of the eight factors were being implemented in their SSR program. Since the teachers were regularly including four of the eight factors, partially including though three of the factors, and not including one of the factors at all, we identified their program as a minimally "stacked for success" program. The four factors the Community School staff implemented strongly were *appeal, conducive environment, non-accountability,* and *distributed time to read.* The three factors which were implemented in a partial fashion were *access to books, encouragement,* and *staff training.* Finally, the factor of *follow-up activities* was missing entirely.

Strong Factors

Appeal Book appeal was incorporated by allowing students to self-select and read any kinds of materials they wished, including magazines, newspapers, and comics. The school library had recently added a large number of high interest, low vocabulary books to the current holdings, and students were encouraged to bring materials that they liked from home or to borrow them from friends or family members.

Conducive Environment A conducive environment was established by providing a physically comfortable area for reading. Students sat at their own desks in air-conditioned and well-lit rooms. The SSR rule for quiet among the readers was strictly enforced. Whenever students became chatty, teachers reminded them that SSR is supposed to be "sustained" and "silent." Doing homework during SSR time was not allowed in favor of asking students to read something purely for pleasure so that they would view the reading environment as supportive and risk-free.

Non-Accountability There were no accountability measures following the SSR period. I saw various forms of Reading Records in the different classrooms, but the teachers indicated that student response was optional. Most students kept records in order to keep their places in their books, although others simply preferred to use bookmarks.

Distributed Time to Read Time to read silently was offered daily in most classes for about twelve to fifteen minutes, representing a "distributed" approach. However, in one class, a novice teacher shared with me that she had been inspired by Krashen's talk to give students SSR time. She had then given her students the opportunity to vote on whether they wanted to read for fifteen minutes each day or for the whole class period on Friday. To veteran teachers, the results of this vote would not have been surprising: the students chose to read for the whole period on Friday. Of course, this translated into a "free time" attitude on the last day of each school week, and the disconcerted young teacher did not see why SSR was not working for her classes. Once we discussed the importance of establishing reading as a habit, she recognized that students should maintain a daily schedule for reading, which would undermine the Friday "party-hardy" attitude and help to make the environment more serious and conducive to reading. Her students then settled down to reading every day.

Weak Factors

Staff Training Staff training was implemented only partially because, although several of the staff members had attended the fall presentation in which teachers were encouraged to develop SSR programs, attention had not been paid to making implementation procedures consistent. In addition, there was no consensus among ESL department members about the value of SSR, in general. Many believed that it would offer valuable benefits to students, while others were uncertain if it would be worth the class time invested. While observing classes at the Community School, I noticed that when students became restless after a few minutes, some teachers shortened the intended twelve-minute SSR time period and began class lessons earlier than planned. This response may have indicated a lack of buy-in on the part of the teachers, since they were not willing to take the additional steps needed to help students become more engaged during the reading period.

Access Access to books was provided by allowing students to utilize materials from existing classroom collections and to visit the school library, which was open five periods a day. Also, the librarian had just purchased a large number of "easy reading" high interest books through Title I funds based on recommendations from teachers. However, though students were offered a wide variety of materials, if they chose from the classroom library, they were not allowed to take the materials home. A box was kept for each class of students; at the end of each period, materials were collected and stored safely away for the next day's reading period. This procedure more than likely negatively impacted students' levels of motivation to read. A student who became inspired by a story or passage during the SSR period could not continue reading at home in the evening—which lessened the reader's chances of developing the reading "habit". Not continuing to read outside of school hours leads to a reduced incentive to find the same book the next day in class. Actually, when we watch students' reading patterns carefully, we see that access to books has a much broader definition than we might at first believe. It includes having books available after school hours, too, in order to maintain the reading interest that has been stimulated during the reading period. Effective reading patterns should reflect a spiral upward, where enthusiasm for a book leads to the choosing of another one, and over time, harder ones, until students are not only hooked on reading but are also proficient lifelong readers.

Encouragement Encouragement to read was offered by asking students to read when they were not reading and reminding them that reading was important. Students were told that their reading would improve if they participated in free reading, but teachers did not share the information about the related "spread of effect" of improved language abilities in spelling, vocabulary, grammar, and writing that accompany improvement in reading. Also, some but not all teachers modeled reading during the SSR time. They often graded papers, wrote assignments on the boards, or took phone calls. This "do as I say and not as I do" attitude can lead students to believe that the free reading idea is just a ploy to keep them quiet and suggests that free reading is not truly important; after all, the teacher isn't doing it, either.

Missing Factors

Follow-up Activities Follow-up activities were not included in any way since regular class activities began when the silent reading periods ended each day. Students were not offered opportunities to share what they had been reading.

Goals of the Research Study

The research goals for this study were similar to the earlier Pilot Study objectives and related to the development of students' comprehension and motivation to read. They included:

1. improved reading comprehension
2. greater enjoyment of pleasure reading
3. more frequent engagement in outside pleasure reading (home reading)
4. utilization of a wider range of pleasure-reading sources

In order to measure achievement of these goals, pretest-posttest forms of the Student Questionnaire were used in conjunction with the pretest-posttest forms of the Stanford Diagnostic Reading Test, or SDRT. (See Appendix J for an example of the Student Pre-Post Questionnaires.) Also, we developed an instrument based on the Estes Attitude Scales (which we were given permission to use with considerable modifications to make it more comprehensible for intermediate ESL students) called the Student Attitude Survey, to assess student perceptions about reading. Having been allotted some release time, I administered all of the pretests within a three-day window of time at both schools during September. Classroom teachers were present during the administrations at the Community School, so there would be no conflict of interest and everyone would have the maximum assurance that tests were administered in a uniform manner. The SSR programs in both schools ran for sixteen weeks (until the end of January), at which time all of the posttest assessments were administered and analyzed.

Results of the Research Study

Improved Reading Comprehension

Scores of the students in both schools increased, but the Home School's average gain in scores on the sixty-point SDRT was 1.67 points higher than the Community School's average gain in scores. However, while this difference was significant, it was only modest. According to the Table of Norms for the SDRT, both groups made approximately ten months of growth in four months. (Note: Though the experimental group averaged almost a two-point raw score increase over the comparison group, their grade-equivalency gain scores were the same. When raw scores approach the middle of the range on the norms table, greater grade equivalency increases are seen per raw score point. Since the comparison group started higher and ended higher, their more modest average growth was represented numerically—in terms of grade equivalency—exactly the same as the experimental group.) (See Appendix K, Table 1.)

Greater Enjoyment of Pleasure Reading

Scores of the students in both schools increased, but the Home School's average gain in scores on the 40-point Student Attitude Survey was 2.01 points higher than the Community School's average gain in scores. (See Appendix K, Table 2.) This difference was significant. (For a breakdown of this survey by school and by item, please refer to Appendix K, Tables 3 and 4.)

More Frequent Engagement in Outside Pleasure Reading (Home Reading)

Scores of the students in the Home School increased, but scores of the students in the Community School actually declined a bit. The Home School's average gain in scores on the four-point portion of the Student Pretest-Posttest Questionnaire was .43 points, but the Community School's average dropped by .04 points. This difference was significant. (See Appendix K, Table 5; for a breakdown of each outside reading category, see Table 6.)

Use of a Wider Range of Pleasure Reading Sources

Scores of the students in both schools increased, but the Home School's average gain in scores on the seven-point portion of the Student Pretest-Posttest Questionnaire was .64 points higher than the Community School's average gain in points. This difference was significant. It is clear that the Home School students used a narrower range of sources at the beginning of the study than the Community School students did, yet the Home School students increased their total number of sources by almost 33 percent, while the Community School made modest gains. (See Appendix K, Table 7 for the numerical results and Table 8 for a breakdown of outside reading sources by category.)

Implications of the Research Study

It is important to recognize that the students in both schools made gains in reading comprehension and increased positive attitudes toward reading. However, the students in the "stacked for success" school program, that is, the one which incorporated all eight of the factors, did better. These gains were supported by statistical evidence.

The greatest gains were made in the area of increased positive attitude toward reading. In my view, how students feel about reading is the most important concern of teachers who are starting a new SSR program. Once students actually start to enjoy reading on a regular basis, reading comprehension logically develops. The fact that there were significant differences between the students' scores in comprehension in the two schools indicates a trend in improvement for the students in the "stacked for success" program that would possibly have been even more considerable if the programs had run for a full year.

If we review the factors that the Community School implemented, we can identify areas that required strengthening. The lack of staff training and follow-up activities could well have lessened the excitement of the SSR program for staff and students alike. Also, the absence of teacher modeling during SSR and the inaccessibility of classroom materials for home reading in the evenings may have contributed to the students' perceptions of reading as a low priority activity. It is interesting to note that while students in both schools made some gains for almost every goal, the one area in which the Community School students made almost no progress was in students' frequency of outside reading. This finding makes sense, given that students had a paucity of easily accessible materials for at-home reading.

The study itself was a fascinating experience, and all of the teachers who participated were capable, motivated people who cared a great deal about their students' progress. At the conclusion of the study, I made a presentation to the faculties of both schools and discussed the findings. Highly professional educators, the teachers who had been involved in developing SSR programs in their classrooms were happy to receive information about the eight factors and how to implement them. Principals at both sites were extremely supportive and offered financial and professional support to their staffs in their ongoing efforts to modify and refine their free reading programs. Of course, I was asked many questions about how to incorporate the factors in practical ways. In the next chapter, I will address some of the issues that these staff members, as well as teachers and administrators from many other schools that I have visited, have raised.

5

Recommendations for Realistic SSR Implementation

At the beginning of this book I made the statement that it is time to stop telling people *that* SSR works and start telling them *how* it works. We know that SSR offers powerful benefits to our student—and that it is a critical component that should be included in our school programs throughout the secondary school years for both English-only and ESL students. Hopefully, the descriptions of the studies that we analyzed, in addition to those we conducted, paint a fairly clear picture of what an effective SSR program should include, but there are still many questions to be answered about how to incorporate the eight Factors for SSR Success in practical ways. The purpose of this chapter is to help you implement a "stacked for success" SSR program in your own classroom or school, even if you have limited resources available. I will also try to answer some of the most frequently-asked questions educators often ask me about specific barriers that they encounter as they begin to implement such programs on their own.

First of all, whether you reveal the SAFE DATE acronym to your students or not, I think it is wise to share the eight components with them. As a teacher, I often develop tunnel vision when I've put a lot of effort into a project, and the last thing I want to hear from anyone is that I need to do more or make it better, just when I think I've done the best I can. However, students often shed light on problems that I haven't noticed—and more important, can usually suggest appropriate and effective ways to solve them. I found that when I told my students about the eight factors, they quickly let me know when I violated any of them. This perspective helped me to be more sensitive to what was happening in my classroom . . . and certainly kept me humble, too. As I discuss the suggestions for implementation, I will include a few of the illuminating observations that my students shared.

Implementing the Factors

Access

Access to interesting reading materials is a critical issue. I can't tell you how many times teachers tell me that SSR doesn't work because the students simply won't bring their books to class. Many people assume it is the students' responsibility to find something they like and to bring it to class for the free reading period. Well, at some point we'd like to see them so involved in reading that they will do this. But, at the beginning of an SSR program, it is up to us to provide the materials that students want to read. As Leonhardt (1997) urges us, sometimes we must be both "creative and persistent" in our search to locate materials (19).

Classroom Libraries Of course, the first places we should stock with reading materials are the classrooms where SSR will occur. Classroom bookshelves, book bins, and spinners are physically closest to the students and therefore most accessible. Sanacore (1992) refers to surrounding students with classroom books as "cluttering up the classrooms," recommending this kind of easy access as a way of tempting students to browse and to read some of the sources. One way to receive money

Figure 5–1. Romi and Wilson head to the class bookshelf to choose new titles for SSR.

to buy classroom materials is to ask your administrator for a small grant through one of the school's funding sources. Since I taught in a Title I program for many years, I often received funding for books through Title I monies. However, there are numerous funding sources available, and the administrators at your schools know what they are. You can easily write a short proposal that justifies your need for reading materials and outlines the program you plan to set up. Then, take it to your administration and ask for support. In all likelihood, you'll get a positive response.

PTA Support Your school PTA is another viable source of funding. Type up a written plan for an SSR program, complete with a rationale; then call your PTA president and ask to be placed on the agenda for the next meeting. Take your plan to the meeting (after sending a copy to your principal) and describe to the parents and teachers what you want to do. Ask them how they might be able to help you. Sometimes they will offer to provide a specific amount of money from their regular budget. Other times they may volunteer to participate in magazine and newspaper drives to help you gather materials. One parent I met at a PTA meeting actually owned a comic book shop. He immediately donated 100 new comic books to my classroom. (You could hear a pin drop for weeks afterward during SSR). If you decide to use donated materials, I would issue a word of caution: set up a small committee of teachers that will be using the books to oversee their selection. Before the materials are placed in classrooms, any inappropriate classroom materials (such as the Swimsuit Edition of *Sports Illustrated* which once found its way into my bungalow and caused an entire period of havoc) should be weeded out. As I told my students after this incident, "If it's something that will cost me my job if the principal sees it, it's out of the question." My students laughed, but they never violated the rule after that.

Community Resources Writing letters to community businesses can also be productive. When you tell business owners that you are seeking funding to buy reading materials for kids, they are usually pleased to be able to help in some way, particularly if you mention their names in the school bulletin or newsletter. Ask for a donation for a magazine subscription or for some specific reading materials that your students would enjoy. Many companies (including Scholastic, Inc., and National Geographic) offer catalogues, which list numerous magazines containing historical and current news; literary selections; and science, math, art, and health articles. You can check the prices of class subscriptions and ask for specific amounts to cover the ones that your class has chosen. I generally had more success when I mentioned the exact figure I needed, which ran from about $20 to $50 a year for a subscription. In addition, sometimes local newspaper companies—partially out of philanthropy and partially due to good business sense—will donate subscriptions to your classrooms so that students will learn to enjoy periodicals and benefit educationally from the information they provide. Of course, they may also become future subscribers, which is a goal that we, as well as the newspaper companies, endorse.

Book Clubs Another wonderful source of new materials is the Book Club. Several types of book club subscriptions are available for young adult readers. Two of the most popular are *Troll*, published by Troll Book Clubs (for upper grades, including middle school and high school) and *Tab*, published by Scholastic, Inc. (for high school). However, *Trumpet 4–6* (published by The Trumpet Club) is geared for upper elementary grades and often includes articles that middle schoolers enjoy and can comprehend more easily, if they need reading materials at lower readability levels. (Addresses of these companies are listed in Chapter 6.) Students can purchase their own materials at reasonable prices, and you can earn bonus points for all of the books they order. The bonus points can then, in turn, be used to redeem other new books for everyone to share. There is nothing as thrilling as receiving a box of new Book Club materials during the middle of a school week. Just opening the box and passing out all of those shiny, colorful new paperbacks generates such enthusiasm that students will want to order again immediately—usually that very day. The passing around of new titles and subsequent keen interest in sharing cannot be matched by any other classroom activity.

Rotation of Materials Next, it's always possible to figure out ways to trade books with other teachers. Some ESL teachers I worked with each bought $500 of new SSR books (approximately 100) at the beginning of the school year. Then, about once a quarter (every ten weeks), they rotated their books. By the end of the year, their students had been exposed to more than $2,000 worth of books (approximately 400), just in their ESL classrooms. Of course, they needed to have a check-out system for the books in order to keep track of what titles were lost during the year, but they apprenticed their students as classroom librarians and worked it out very satisfactorily. They ordered library check-out cards from the district warehouse and taped pockets into the backs of the reading materials. When students wanted to check out books, they put their names, the dates, and book titles on the cards, which they then handed to the class "librarian." When they were finished with the book, they returned them to the class librarian, who crossed their names off the cards and replaced them in the book pockets. This way, at any given time, the librarian knew which titles students had checked out and could start waiting lists if others were interested in the same book. The system also placed a measure of responsibility upon the students to make sure to return the books. If books were lost, students were given the option of paying for replacing the specific titles or bringing in other books to add to the classroom collection. Interestingly, while my students thought this was a "fair deal," they were also concerned that irresponsible students might donate books that weren't as exciting as the ones that were lost. Therefore, they kept a poster in the corner of the classroom entitled "Kinds of Books We Want" and encouraged students to donate books within the most popular genres. Mystery books were probably listed the most often, but romance always came in a clear second.

Neighborhood Searches One seventh grade middle school class had a contest to collect more books for their classroom libraries. They asked students to search their neighborhoods to collect books, magazines, and other reading materials. Then, the students who brought the most books to the school were given " pretend" money to use at a school auction, where many creative gifts such as hamburger and ice-cream coupons donated by local companies, plus a couple of CD and video certificates (given by the PTA), were available. Activities like this can be highly energizing because, although not all of the materials donated can ultimately be used in the classrooms, the importance of reading is highlighted and publicized to everyone on the school campus and in the neighboring communities.

Book Fairs Another way to bring inspiring new titles to your campus is to become involved in setting up a Book Fair at your school. Many companies do an excellent job of providing a wide range of appealing titles for students to purchase during fairs on campus. They will come to your campus and set up attractive book displays as a forum for selling materials and creating interest in reading. Then, you can advertise, advertise, advertise! A motivational, social, and lucrative activity is to invite parents to the school during a Book Fair so that they can purchase the books that intrigue their young people. Such fairs offer students opportunities to see new titles that the libraries may not yet possess and to make available the most popular series and classics that students have not had opportunities to purchase elsewhere. Students can hold the books, turn the pages, and read a little—just to see if they want to add any of them to their personal collections. Prices are usually reasonable at these fairs, and more than likely, each student will want to buy at least one! I would also suggest that if you have some special monies (e.g., from the Student Cabinet), you can buy books for students who might not otherwise be able to afford them. A perfect way to influence young persons to become readers is to buy them some appealing books of their own.

Getting parents involved in seeing exciting reading materials, though, is half the battle. Adults are usually not reluctant to purchase "fun" reading materials when teachers are recommending Home Reading, and their teens are so excited about getting them. My daughter's eighth grade class had a Book Fair during the week of Open House, and I'm sure I didn't leave that campus without spending at least twenty-five dollars. The spirit was infectious, and the message was loud and clear: books are wonderful, and reading is important!

Another benefit to having a Book Fair is that you can allow your students to become involved in the setting up of displays, in developing creative ways to do the advertising, and in collecting the incoming funds (with adult supervision, of course). This makes the Book Fair project their own, and when the final sales figures are published, they take great pride in having supported their school. At the secondary level, we become so accustomed to fund-raisers such as car washes and garage sales that it is refreshing to see a focus not just on earning money, but also on highlighting the importance of books. The money raised can then be funneled back into school reading collections. A PTA president I recently talked to said that after the very successful book fair at her school (at which many students and parents purchased books), all of the money earned was devoted to buying materials for the school library and for teachers who had submitted special requests for new titles to shore up their classroom libraries.

School Libraries In addition to using classroom materials, it is important to discover ways to get students to visit the school library. Consider asking your librarian to do a special presentation for specific classes so that they know where to find their favorite kinds of books. I shared the results of our Student Interest Inventory with our librarian. She was kind enough to have some popular titles ready ahead of time for the students to see when they came in. I later discovered that it was easier when I worked out an arrangement with the librarian in the fall so that three or four times during the year, we spent an entire class period seeing what was new in the school library and helping students find popular or special books that we didn't have in our classroom. It's important, however, that the time students spend in the library allows them to get involved in selecting books *and* reading them. In her study of nine schools in the Los Angeles area, Pucci (1998) found that when students visited the library as a whole class, most of the activities consisted of "checking in" the students and "checking out" the books. There was very little time for browsing and almost no time at all for real reading.

It's also critical to know the library schedule so that you can send older students to the library on their own when they are seeking a new book. Make sure that your students know the procedures for checking out free reading books so that they can do it quickly and easily. I often sent one or two students to the school library during our SSR periods, and they returned by the end of the fifteen minute period, new books in hand for Home Reading or for SSR the following day.

Community Libraries Finally, familiarize your students with the community library. A field trip is a real treat and can be the vehicle through which students see the vast array of choices that are available to them. If a visit is not a practical option, older students should be shown how to fill out applications for library cards (the library will send them to you) and given directions to the nearest locations. At Open House or Back-to-School Night, encourage parents to offer their teens transportation to the library for checking out pleasure reading books. I even suggested to my students' parents that they consider purchasing magazine subscriptions, if possible: *Seventeen, Teen, YM, People* and *Teen People, Sports Illustrated* and *Sports Illustrated for Kids, Road and Driver, Car Craft, Entertainment Weekly, Newsweek, Time,* and other readily available titles offer motivational reading fare for adolescents. During special events when parents come to your class, have several of these titles displayed prominently and talk with them about how much the students enjoy reading them when they arrive each month. Surprisingly, students and parents often are not aware that they can find periodicals in the public libraries, believing that they are special kinds of materials that must be purchased, rather than borrowed. In her interviews with fourteen ESL high school students, Constantino (1998) found that most of the students were not familiar with the concept of finding newspapers or magazines at the library. Said one of the students, Pablo, in amazement, when asked about his feeling toward the periodicals in the school library, "Hey, they have magazines and other stuff there? I did not know about that!" (60).

Sometimes we need to be proactive and encourage students to investigate community or school libraries. In a study by Ramos and Krashen (1998), teachers took 104 students to the neighborhood library on a monthly basis during school time. They were allowed to explore the library, share books, and not feel constrained by the need to be quiet. Sixty-seven percent of the youngsters asked to be taken back to the library after the first visit; and only three weeks after this visit, students reported that they read more, that reading was easier, and that they (still) wanted to return to the library.

Other Sources Book and magazine sources are also available on the internet; but students need parental permission and supervision to locate and purchase materials if they are interested in accessing books via this route. In general, the goal is to provide a book flood so students have access to a wide range of interesting reading materials. Asking them to locate the materials on their own will only result in frustration for you and for them. When you start to notice that your students are finding their own reading materials, you will know that they are on the road to becoming habitual readers.

Appeal

I once knew a librarian who read every new book that she ordered for the library in an effort to make sure that the children read quality literature. She always had the most current knowledge of the newest Caldecott Medal winners, the Young Reader Medal winners, and the Newberry Medal winners; and her library shelves were lined with all of the award-winning titles. Yet, when I asked the students at her school how often they visited the library to check out a book just for fun, they replied, "never" or "only once in while." Their reason was that the library just "didn't have enough interesting books—the kind we like."

One writer points out that by the middle school years children usually have definite opinions about the types of books they like to read, and frequently, adults seem unable to identify these high-appeal materials (Everett 1987). Highlighting this idea, she notes that only a small percentage of books recommended by the critics in the *School Library Journal* receive favorable recommendations by the students themselves. In other words, students know what they like better than we do.

Interest Surveys Since self-selection is a crucial part of SSR, it is worthwhile to spend some time determining how to offer appealing reading materials to students. Various researchers have noted that learners' spontaneous interests need to be reflected in the materials that are presented (Hafiz and Tudor 1989, Clary 1991). One way to be sure that this occurs is to survey students' interests before reading materials are chosen. You can administer an interest inventory or hold a discussion with the students about what they like to read. (I like to do both; shy students are sometimes reluctant to share their thoughts with the whole class.) Jimi, a teacher at Upland High School, developed a Reader's Survey, which guided her selections of course materials and gave her much-needed insight into her students' attitudes about reading, in general. (See Appendix L for an example.)

One middle school teacher told me that she offered her students "wish lists," on which they identified three books they would like to have in the classroom. She promised to buy at least one of their choices the next time she purchased SSR books. When the books arrived, students of course looked for "their books" and instantly felt a sense of ownership toward them.

Book Lists Another way to find materials that teens appreciate is to use book lists that are published specifically with teens in mind. For example, *More Teens' Favorite Books*, published by the International Reading Association, includes books appropriate for young-adult readers, complete with bibliographic information, annotations, and author/title indexes. Entries are grouped by type or genre of publication to make books of particular interest easy to find. IRA also releases a *Young Adult Choice* pamphlet each fall, which lists the most popular selections of the previous year (and only costs about a dollar). Another excellent source of interesting materials for adolescents can be found in a book entitled 99 *Ways to Get Kids to Love Reading* (Leonhardt 1997). The author provides a section called "100 Books They'll Love" in which she divides books by genres and identifies titles especially suited to older students. Kathleen O'Dean's *Great Books for Girls* (1997) also offers an entire section, thematically-organized, on appealing titles for older readers. Other excellent sources like these are published by the American Library Association and the National Council of Teachers of English and are listed in Chapter 6.

Variety of Genres In order to offer enough choices to suit all students, a free reading program should include a wide variety of different genres. Frequently-mentioned additions to such programs are paperbacks; periodicals such as magazines and newspapers; picture books, story books; tradebooks; and non-fiction books of all kinds, including biographies. I was pleased to find out about a publishing company entitled Discovery Enterprises, Ltd., which has a large number of historical fiction and biographies, since many of my students were history buffs. Keeping on the mailing lists of such publishers is an effective way to provide your students with genres they like and to help yourself stay abreast of new books on the market.

One popular source is what Krashen (1993) refers to as "light reading," which includes comic books and teen romances, materials that would typically not be found on literary critics' lists of books that young people should read. As Ujiie and Krashen (1996) found in their study on comic book reading, the comic book readers they studied read more frequently for pleasure and enjoyed reading more than non-comic book readers. Such light reading fare can be considered a conduit to more demanding reading and should therefore be part of the options we provide in school. Because students are told what to read throughout most of their school lives and therefore often see reading as a school task, free reading programs call for a large variety of choices "in order to avoid the depressing contrast between what appears as exciting home reading and the dull reading fare of school" (Carlsen and Sherrill 1988, 37).

Unfortunately, some parents do not agree that students should be able to read lighter material. I have come into contact with some who absolutely refuse to let their children read anything unless it is parent-approved. One fifteen-year-old student in my class was only allowed to read from the *Bible* or from the encyclopedia. When she came home with a *Seventeen* magazine that I had given her, I received a harsh phone call from her mother who threatened to drop her from my class if I continued to let her read such "trash." The girl came to school the next day in tears and handed back the precious copy of the magazine. Two years later, when she was a senior, I saw her sitting in the quad, reading. She had a stack of magazines that she had purchased herself. She smiled at me and said, "I can read anything I want to now. I'm an adult." Think of the reading time she missed out on between her sophomore and senior years! Perhaps if her mother had let her read the materials she craved earlier, she might have been engaged in more sophisticated reading when I saw her in the quad. The point is that students will find

Calvin and Hobbes   by Bill Watterson

Figure 5–2 Calvin and Hobbes © 1989 Watterson. Reprinted with permission of Universal Press Syndicate. All rights reserved.

what they want to read, no matter what we deny them. Providing a wide range of material in our classes ensures that there will be something for everyone.

Range of Readability Levels Different levels of readability and length also contribute to book appeal. Shorter books place less strain on learners' concentration and are more likely to be picked up and read at odd moments. Consider keeping a small set of short-story anthologies on your desk for the days when you see lethargic readers, who need something they can get into and finish quickly. A favorite on my desk was *Athletic Shorts*, by Chris Crutcher, a short-story anthology about real teenagers facing challenges and doing their best. Students often derive a feeling of achievement from completing a whole story or a short book in a couple of days.

However, since reading levels in each class will vary, more difficult, as well as easier works, should be available to meet students' needs. Ironically, sometimes a good reader will choose an "easy" book, while a less capable reader will choose a more difficult one. As Barbe and Abbott (1975) indicate, it is "not necessary to read material at any exact level" (54). Interestingly, however, the books young people choose on their own are usually more difficult than those assigned by their teachers (Krashen 1996). This may be because of the higher levels of motivation associated with self-selection.

It may also be helpful for you to consult with the reading specialist at your school to find out how to assess the range of your students' reading abilities. I gave the Gates-MacGinitie Reading Test to all of my classes just to get a feel for what my students' independent reading levels were. That way, I had a starting point for selecting materials within each class's range. Also, if you are aware of a student's particular interests, it helps to know what materials to suggest that are at approximately the right reading level. I did find, though, that when my students were committed to a particular genre or series, they could often read books one or two years above what their test results indicated. For example, many of my female students who tested at the third or fourth grade reading level managed to handle the *Sweet Valley High* stories by Francine Pascal (fifth–sixth grade level) very well.

In order to determine the readability levels of your materials, there are several things you can do. Some books have the interest level (IL) and the readability level (RL) listed on the back, which is handy. Just remember that the interest level will be higher than the reading level for these books if they are considered "easy readers." Also, you can do a quick assessment of a book by using a readability formula, found in most reading-methods textbooks. Easier, though, is to buy the Fry Readability Scale (published by Contemporary Books), which has simple directions and costs less than ten dollars. However, the scale only gives you baseline information using a mathematical formula derived from the average syllable count and number of sentences in selected passages. It does not take your students' background knowledge or the complexity of the author's style into account, two factors which directly influence the comprehensibility of the text. I once gave my high school students a ghost story entitled "Pipe Smoke" which, according to the Fry Formula, was written at the sixth grade level. Though the ESL students I was working with could generally handle sixth grade material, many had problems understanding the plot of the story. They had very little schema for the horror-story genre and had difficulty following the events, which to them seemed implausible. In other words, it's important to know your students' background experiences because appropriate reading level alone does not always guarantee success.

I also found that keeping catalogues from publishers in a file for easy reference was helpful in numerous instances when I was selecting materials for particular students who had made special requests. Once you are on the mailing lists of a number of publishers, you will receive new catalogues automatically each year. Then, if you need to know the readability level of a book you have purchased from a company, you can call the 800 number and ask. The information is usually available from a customer-service representative.

Another approach to take is to order periodicals that are written for specific grade-level readers. For example, Scholastic, Inc., offers a wide range of magazines for youngsters—all with grade levels listed. My students especially enjoyed *Science World* and *Choices*, which are written at high school interest levels. The International Reading Association also publishes a compendium of periodical titles, listed alphabetically, entitled *Magazines for Kids and Teens*. Not only does it have age and subject indexes, but it also offers a section on how to use the book—and an inspiring forward by Jim Trelease, the well-known author of the *Read-Aloud Handbook*. National Geographic, too, offers wonderful periodicals in the areas of social studies, current events, nature, ecology, and geography. Easier reading materials include *National Geographic World*, but more advanced periodicals are available, too.

Read-along Books and Tapes One exciting way to support readers who can benefit from repeated readings is to offer read-along tapes with favorite books. I purchased a series of twenty-two short books and read-along tapes from the Sundown Collection, published by New Reader's Press, and then offered students opportunities to use a listening center with headphones during SSR. Genres within the series included sports, mysteries, classic myths and legends, informational books on self-help topics, and science—all written at readability levels my ESL students could handle. When students selected books that interested them, but felt they were not comprehending the stories well enough, they could always rewind and re-read. The same opportunities existed for those who simply enjoyed hearing a story more than once or who felt more successful with the reading process during a second or third reading.

Attractive Covers Book appeal can also be enhanced by making sure that the appearance of your reading materials is attractive. In his reform-school study, Fader (1976) noted that the paperbacks in his school became "invitations to possession." He documented their effectiveness in motivating the young boys to read by tabulating how many of them were stolen each week, having been stuffed into readers' pockets (80). In my classroom, I, too, found that colorful paperbacks seemed to be more enticing than hardbound books, even the perma-bound kind. Also, SSR went more smoothly when I displayed new magazine issues and dropped several copies of the daily newspaper on the center table of the room. The need for an environment which is filled with many kinds of authentic reading materials—what we refer to as a "print-rich environment"—is not limited to emergent readers but exists for readers of all ages and levels. Having a large number of inviting reading materials readily accessible is the first step toward encouraging students to want to read. Then, as Van Jura (1984) reminds us, "The key point is to accept the students' reading choices" (541).

Good Student-Book Matches I must say a word here about matching students with books. One of the most common problems that teachers report to me is that students cannot find books that they like. If we simply put young people in rooms with many reading materials, there is no assurance that matches will be made. Students often need the personal touch; they require that a caring teacher or other adult talk with them about their interests and help to recommend something they might like. Being asked to choose something on their own can be a frustrating and futile experience. Personally, however, I agree with Sherman (1996), a veteran seventh grade reading/language arts teacher and a past chair of IRA's Special Interest Group on Adolescent Literature (SIGNAL), who recommends helping only when help is asked for. She recounts an instance in her own classroom when she had to "bite her lip" in order to wait for a student (who was foundering in her quest to find intrinsically motivating literature and settling for light romances) to request her input. When the student finally did, a match was made and the student was on her way to becoming a prolific reader. However, those of us who deal with adolescents understand Sherman's observation that if she had charged in with an "unsought recommendation," the student would probably still be clinging to her old familiar choices of materials "out of spite" (511).

It is advisable, though, to give reluctant students an opening for telling you they want some help. Even after several weeks, when SSR had become a regular part of our curriculum, I occasionally noticed students in my classroom who were distracted during the reading period. After it was over, I would approach them to have a short conversation. Almost always, they admitted that they were having trouble finding a "good book." We would talk about what a good book for them might be—and by the next SSR period I would hand them a couple of choices that I thought might match their requests. The first time was not always the charm, but it certainly helped the students and me to get closer to something that would satisfy them; and the personal attention the students received was worth a great deal on its own. At least they got the message that I considered their reading important enough to take my own time to help them find interesting books. I will say a bit more about this kind of student-book match in the section on encouragement. For now, it is enough to point out that the role of the teacher in making books appealing for students is an active one—and with respect to certain students, more active sometimes than others.

Jody, the tutor for a reluctant eighth grade reader, took her tutee to the bookstore after school one day to purchase some books. When the middle school student chose a *Mary Kate and Ashley* mystery book, Jody was surprised, thinking the subject matter was too juvenile for her. It turned out that the book was written at her independent reading level—fourth grade—and the student was so encouraged by being able to read and comprehend it that she not only read the book completely in a couple of evenings, but asked Jody if they could immediately start on a second one in the same series. This newly-inspired reader could not be considered "reluctant" anymore!

Conducive Environment

A great deal of attention has been paid to the idea of providing an environment that is conducive to free reading. It is logical that when readers are in comfortable, quiet surroundings, they will be more motivated to start reading and to sustain it. Therefore, there are some basic characteristics of the reading environment that are required.

Comfortable Surroundings First of all, students must feel completely at ease. The physical characteristics of the reading environment are significant in promoting this feeling. Readers must have, at the very least, enough room to sit at desks or tables in the classroom without being cramped. SSR in a science classroom can be deadly if students are seated on stools beside sinks or bunsen burners. They should be able to put their elbows on the table and their feet on the floor. Heat or air conditioning is also important when weather conditions merit their use. It's important for us to be aware of the conditions of a classroom and to make improvements when we can. (Once when our air conditioning failed, I took my entire class out to the senior grove to sit beneath some trees during SSR.) If ventilation is not satisfactory, talk to your principal and ask for a work order to be submitted. Sometimes changes can be made if we simply take an active role.

If the environment contains some homey accoutrements, then the atmosphere can be even more pleasant and add to the level of student comfort. Morrow (1982) has documented that young children use library corners more when pillows, easy chairs, and carpets are part of the reading environment. In my classroom, too, I found that when I ordered circular tables instead of individual student desks, my students relaxed more easily. There was a sense of community that didn't exist when they were seated in neat, tidy rows. It's true that I had to submit a written rationale for the funding to get the special tables, but once the room was set up and other reading teachers saw how comfortable the environment was, the administration provided circular tables for their classes, too.

In some classrooms there are easy chairs, study carrells, rugs, and oversized pillows—or what Gambrell (1978) calls "great nooks and crannnies" (331). It is important to remember that for some students, especially those sensitive to stimuli, these special kinds of locations may sometimes be necessary (Barbe and Abbott 1975).

I know of a wonderful school in Mount Baldy, California, where students can do their SSR in "treehouses." These are built inside the classrooms and contain pillows and a wide variety of reading materials. I'll never forget my first visit there during SSR, where elementary and middle school students were stretched out in various positions in their treehouses as they avidly read their books. Such creative kinds of reading centers offer students a measure of comfort that they might not even have at home—and provide an incentive for reading in a fun and different environment.

Other researchers have suggested adding students' art work, colorful posters, book jackets and mobiles (Gambrell 1971). Clary (1991) recommends providing the teacher with a footstool, lamp, plants, and pictures for a homey feel. She maintains that when we give children comfortable spots to read, "an atmosphere that shouts the important of reading" is established (343). The American Library Association publishes excellent catalogues filled with posters, stickers, book marks and other incentives that promote reading, and their prices are reasonable. Other reading inducements for bulletin boards and walls are available in the *Upstart* catalogue (published by Upstart in Wisconsin) and the *Poster Extravaganza* catalog, published by the Perfection Learning Corporation in Iowa, which features posters related to favorite book titles.

For many of us, the basic physical characteristics of our classrooms may remain unalterable. However, some adjustments can be made to create an atmosphere that is more pleasant and therefore more conducive to free reading. Judy, a friend of mine who teaches at-risk eleventh and twelfth graders, managed to buy an old over-stuffed sofa that she put in the back of her classroom for students to use during SSR. (The Student Cabinet at her school raised the $35 for it.) She also placed flowers around the room and put up posters of pop stars engaged in reading. Another teacher bought bean bag chairs with a special grant she received, and placed them in a reading corner. Then, at her request, some of her students' fathers came into her class one weekend and made extra bookshelves to house the students' growing classroom collection of books.

Structure for Reading Part of putting students at ease emotionally, as well as physically, comes from creating a structure for reading so that students know what to expect during free reading periods. Often it takes some time for the programs to get going, and there may be "minor chaos" at first (Greaney 1970). But the students shortly become accustomed to the various procedures involved. Also, part of any free reading program is self-pacing, which means that the students read at rates that are comfortable for them; there is no specific deadline for finishing a book (Sartain 1960). Without the necessity to compete with other readers, the reading time can be a relaxing and enjoyable experience for learners. Jones (1978) has even characterized this kind of SSR time for some students as a much-needed and quite valuable "20 minute vacation" (102).

Low-Risk Atmosphere The risk-free aspect of the reading environment cannot be emphasized enough. Several teachers I've heard of play soft music during the reading period to help students unwind. I found that, in order to feel truly at ease, students also needed to know that their reading selections would not be judged or laughed at by other students, so I asked students to bring in grocery bags to make book covers. Ostensibly, the covers were to protect the books, but I knew that providing them for everyone also ensured that students' self-selected reading materials remained private.

Not all students are primarily concerned about what their peers might think, however. Some simply want to find materials they enjoy. I once spoke to an eleventh grade ESL student who was reading a Dr. Seuss book in his reading class. His teacher, Jan, had provided lots of short, entertaining materials for students who were having trouble sticking to longer books. This young man was laughing aloud at the silly, repetitive verses, and he told me that he enjoyed the book because it was "funny and easy to understand." Though many high-school students would not want to be seen reading Dr. Seuss stories, this student felt comfortable reading what he liked—and what he could comprehend! (His reading level in English was second or third grade.) His teacher was a wise woman who knew the importance of supporting her students' reading selections in a nurturing environment.

Quiet, Sacred Time Quiet is certainly a necessary condition for SSR. As Wiscont (1990) points out, "Many young people lack a quiet place to read" in their home lives (10). Often, reading time in school is their only escape from the distractions of the outside world. The McCracken (1971) students said they liked SSR "because it is quiet," with many indicating that it was the only quiet time in their entire day (582). As I mentioned earlier in this book, my own students began calling our SSR time their "bubble time" when no one else could enter their world—and they were distraught when others threatened to pop it. The need for uninterrupted time is essential if students are to engage in the reading process for increasingly longer periods of time.

One way to ensure that the atmosphere during SSR is quiet (after explaining to students why they should not talk during the free reading period, of course) is to alert the main office that the first fifteen minutes of class time is inviolable except in the case of an emergency. You can also put a sign on the outside of your door that says, "SSH . . . We are reading," or something similar. Ask the office staff not to put through phone calls to you during the first part of each class and not to send messengers, either. If office monitors come into your class, ask them to sit down and read a book until the SSR time is over. (The students might not return ever again—or, they might come back every day!) If your students ask you questions when you are reading, tell them that you would be happy to answer them after SSR and then immediately go back to your book. In other words, make the SSR time truly sacred.

Encouragement

Almost all of us who are avid readers remember someone who encouraged us to read in some way when we were younger. Sometimes it was a parent, a teacher, a brother or sister, a grandparent, or a friend who lent us books, gave us books as gifts, or read to us.

Often, these memories included visions of enjoyable cozy winter days or warm spring afternoons curled up with a book—and perhaps even something good to eat.

I recall that I ate Hostess cupcakes when I read my way through the Nancy Drew series, for example, but others have shared that they relate reading to cookies or popcorn or even pickles. The point is that we saw reading as something fun, a pleasurable activity apart from the grind of typical school tasks. Unfortunately, not all of our students share our perspective.

Encouraging children to read is a critical issue for us today in the age of movies, videos, and computer games. In fact, it is of such concern that one author has written a book about it for parents: *Keeping Kids Reading: How to Raise Avid Readers in the Video Age* (Leonhardt 1996). In it, she discusses how difficult it is to urge students to reach for books as a source of enjoyment when there are so many other entertaining choices to pursue. That is why offering SSR in schools is absolutely essential. Students need to become aware of the stimulation and satisfaction that free reading offers and stop equating it with school work. This change in student perspective can only happen if we have staff members at schools who are committed to the value of reading and to the development of free reading programs.

Adult Modeling Staff members can portray their enthusiasm for reading in a number of ways. It has been demonstrated that teacher modeling has a positive effect on students' reading behavior (Wheldall and Entwhistle 1988), so it is important that all of the adults in the classroom read during SSR. This is because students need to see that reading is a valuable activity, not simply be told that it is (Gambrell 1978; Mork 1972; Cardanelli 1992). One very interesting experiment that I tried with my students was to move from behind my "big teacher's desk" (Atwell 1987) out into the classroom arena. There, I would sit in the place of an absent student and read with my class during SSR. Somehow, being there while I was reading blurred the teacher-student lines and therefore erased the feeling that reading was something only students do. My class got down to reading more quickly, stayed engaged longer, and was much quieter when I was reading in their midst. This experience supports Smith's (1988b) assertion that "children will endeavor to understand and engage in anything they see adults doing, provided the adults demonstrate enjoyment and satisfaction in doing it" (201).

Another positive benefit of modeling during reading is that students become interested in the books that the teacher is reading. Janet Allen (1995) tells of starting to read Mazer's novel, *When the Phone Rang*, during independent reading. Afterwards, three of her students decided to read it, too, their interest piqued by her choice. I once had a list of ten students waiting to read a Jackie Onassis biography that I had selected for SSR. It is clear that the impact of teachers' reading choices on student selections can be very strong. This is why, as Sherman (1996) suggests, teachers need to be avid readers of Young Adult (YA) books. She notes that "seeing a teacher reading 'their' books is far more powerful for students than being told reading's important" (59). If the students believe the teacher reads avidly, they'll be more apt to share their opinions about the titles the teacher hasn't read yet.

Active Teacher Roles Encouragement to read also includes helping students to make matches with books. I addressed this issue briefly in the section on book appeal, but it merits a few additional comments here. Many people view SSR as an activity during which the teacher takes a passive role—and in fact, I know some teachers who have even been accused of not doing their jobs when the students are simply reading. But, linking young people with books that will "hook" them is an active task. We need knowledge about current books that are available for our students' interests, grades, and reading levels. Sometimes we must even haunt garage sales, book warehouse clearances, and used book counters in libraries and book stores in order to find the right books for reluctant readers—or to extend the reading interests of our more prolific readers.

One of my special memories is of a tenth grader who had read every *Hardy Boys* book in my classroom and the school library. I asked my daughter if she would share her *Nancy Drew* mystery collection with him, and he promptly read every book she owned, as well. Then he scoured the school library for any remaining series titles he still hadn't read. By the end of eleventh grade, he had graduated to Ian Fleming novels.

Not only can teachers help students to find interesting books, but we can sometimes even connect them to reading materials that will impact their lives at a critical time. One high school boy whose father had left the family when he was young was struggling to deal with his father's absence. I suggested that he might like to read *Flour Babies* by Anne Fine, the story of a boy who comes to terms with his own father's abandonment through a role-play activity as the father of a "flour baby" in a class experiment. His question to me after reading the book led me to believe that the match had been a good one. He asked, as he handed the book back to me, "Do you have another one like this?" I gave him *Maitland's Kid* by Ann Schraff, a short but intriguing novel about a father-son relationship, which developed many years after the boy had been abandoned.

One comment that my students made to me several weeks after the semester started during our formal study was that they would appreciate having the classroom books organized by genre on the shelves. They felt they could more quickly find what they wanted—and even explore new areas more easily—if the materials were arranged in categories. Of course, I recognized that I should have thought of this earlier, but the students were so pleased that they had come up with the idea on their own that they participated in the reorganization of the bookshelves far more excitedly than they would have if I had suggested it. The classroom "librarians" and some of the class members agreed to help, and for several weeks we shared ideas about what genres particular books might fall into. My students learned that genres can overlap, and they also felt quite sophisticated when they were able to identify new books by genre, usually by reading the excerpts on the backs, the introductions to the books themselves, or by associating a book type with its author. Widening their scope of choices by informing them about different genres served as encouragement for many of them to explore areas and topics they hadn't known existed.

Parent and Administrative Support It is also important to bring administrators and parents into the act of encouraging students to read. Some suggestions have been made about ways in which the principal of the school can become involved. Davis (1992) remarks that among the various ways a principal can exercise leadership in the area of reading skills, acting as a reading role model is one of the most effective. She recounts the case of a principal in Illinois who went to a different classroom every day and selected a student; the student then brought a favorite book to the office and read from it to the principal. The principal listened, discussed the reading with the child, and then modeled reading from the student's book. The child returned to class wearing a badge that said, "I read to the principal today." While this would probably not be a realistic activity for a secondary school, the interaction of the principal with students is an idea that can be a powerful motivator. What we did at my school was to invite the principal to read with us during SSR. Once in awhile, he would simply "visit," and he would join us in reading at the beginning of class. The only missing element was the follow-up discussion. If I were to do it again, I would ask him to tell the class a little bit about the book he was reading and to ask the students questions about what they were reading.

To include parents in the free reading effort, one school in Chicago set aside a twenty-minute minimum recreational reading period at home. Parents filled out a "Parent Pledge" to provide the time (Vandevier 1992). Actually, it is not difficult to send home some kind of a Home Reading sheet which parents can sign. During parent meetings, you can explain how important it is for their sons and daughters to be doing pleasure reading at home. Simply keep in mind that it is not what they read, or how many books they read, but that they do read on a regular basis. If you give parents some guidelines (e.g., fifteen–twenty minutes per evening, five nights a week) and enlist their support, they will usually be happy to support you. The Outside Pleasure Reading sheet that I sent home each Monday (and collected the following Monday) had a space for a parent signature. The point was not so much to prove that the students had actually read but to reinforce to the families how important reading at home was. (See Appendix G for an example of the sheet.) Though I am sure that some parents signed it without being certain that their teenagers ever read a word, the act of signing helped them to recognize that reading was something positive. Several parents actually thanked me for instigating the Home Reading practice. They were able to make agreements with their youngsters about turning off the television or video games for a period of time each evening during Home Reading time—and on Sunday evenings, they would sign the Outside Pleasure Reading slips. On Monday mornings, when we had time to do short book talks, many more students volunteered to participate than they had before Home Reading had become a pattern.

Some of the teachers in the Glendale Unified School District believed so strongly in parent participation that they created a Parent Survey to send home. (See Appendix M for an example of the survey.) The survey included questions about their youngsters' interests, pleasure reading habits, and reading/writing activities done in the home. The survey became part of their portfolio system, so that the information could be passed along from one teacher to another throughout the student's high school experience. In this way, the teachers were able to identify patterns in students' literacy experiences and communicate with parents about ways they could provide support.

Staff members and administrators on your campus who are not involved in the SSR process themselves can also help. One school in Burbank, California, in which the SSR time was offered only during ESL and English classes, cleverly brought the content area teachers into the SSR act. The ESL and English teachers asked the content-area teachers to spend a few moments each day in class discussing the books the students were reading during language arts classes. This way, even though students weren't actually doing free reading in the content-area classes, the importance of reading, in general, was reinforced. Some of the content teachers even talked with the students about their own favorite books and made recommendations for further reading across content-area genres.

Reading as Its Own Incentive A final consideration to address when encouragement is incorporated into a free reading program is the issue of rewards. Kohn (1993) argues that at any age, rewards are less effective than intrinsic motivation for promoting effective learning. He compares adults who love their work (and who do a better job than those goaded with artificial incentives) to children who are more likely to be optimal learners if they are interested in what they are learning. Although some teachers believe that incentive programs which offer rewards (such as pizza and admission tickets to theme parks) have been beneficial at their schools, this may be because such programs have prompted students to begin reading in the first place, in the absence of any other kinds of encouragement. Instead, however, if we design effective SSR programs, which set the structure for creating "a caring community in the classroom . . . where children work together to make decisions"

(Kohn 1993, 255), these kinds of rewards won't be necessary because students will experience the intrinsic satisfaction of pleasure and success.

Kohn (1998) discusses the "bait and switch" approach, in which we use rewards at first to lure students into reading . . . and then fade them out later. He explains that the introduction of an extrinsic motivator immediately changes the whole gestalt—the way a child looks at herself, the way she looks at the person offering the reward, and the way she looks at the task. The more someone is rewarded for doing something (or doing it well), the less interest that person is likely to have in whatever he or she was rewarded for doing. What matters, then, is not the amount but the type of motivation involved—whether the child is encouraged to see reading as something gratifying in its own right.

In his review of ten studies on reading incentives, McQuillan (1997), too, found that none of the studies show any clearly positive effect on reading that can be attributed solely to the use of rewards. When we consider, then, how best to encourage our students to read, we should opt for putting more effort into developing SSR programs that are "stacked for success" than into offering coupons, tickets, stickers, and stars.

Staff Training

Staff training is another aspect of free reading program-planning that must be addressed. When staff members understand the philosophy underlying a teaching method they are implementing, it is more likely that they will be committed more fully to the implementation process. Ganz and Theofield (1974) observe that program planners should find faculty members who "feel as strongly as they do that SSR should be started and are willing to take their lumps to make it happen" (614).

In my opinion, there will always be some staff members who already believe in the necessity for SSR and some who will argue against it, feeling that it detracts from much-needed teaching time and content-area curricula. If you can invite a speaker to your campus who has been involved in a successful SSR program and who has some statistics to show the staff members, you will have a better chance of having the nay-sayers listen. Some of the speakers might be well-known researchers who make these kinds of presentations to single schools or whole districts. Others could include administrators or teachers involved in SSR programs at local schools who might be willing to share their stories with your staff.

I was once invited to a Southern California school that had tried SSR for one year. The program was school-wide, so the staff and students stopped at the same time each day and read. Of course, because not every class of students had a collection of books (e.g., the P.E. students in gym), students were asked to bring their own reading materials. Some of the teachers on the staff were disgruntled about using classroom time for students to read, and often the rules for SSR time were not followed. In fact, in some classes, no reading was done at all. After one year of total frustration on the part of the SSR supporters, I was invited to make a presentation to the staff about the eight factors for SSR success. Afterward, the English Department volunteered to offer free reading in their classes for the following year—and to implement the eight factors to the best of their ability. They simply asked that the rest of the staff support them in their efforts and act as resource people for the students who wanted recommendations for content-area books. I recently spoke with one of the English teachers, who said that the school is very pleased with their program now and plans to continue it next year, as well.

No matter what kind of program you want to implement—whole school, where everyone reads at a given time—or in particular classrooms, it is important for the entire staff to believe in the benefits of SSR and wholeheartedly support its implementation.

Non-Accountability

One of the earliest rules of SSR (which we observed to hold true in the studies we analyzed, as well) was that after the free reading period, there should be no reports or records of any kind. As McCracken (1971) puts it, "Nothing is required initially, or the reluctant readers do not participate" (522). Adding to this idea, he explains that poor readers can make mistakes without worrying, since no one watches them or will catch them making pronunciation errors during silent reading. Therefore, they will not be embarrassed, shamed or ridiculed for failing to demonstrate competence.

Unfortunately, many teachers feel they should check to be sure that students are comprehending what they read. Consider the ubiquitous book report, which is designed to make students accountable for reading a book and showing in some way (some methods being more creative than others) that they understand it. After all, for much of the school day, the emphasis is on continuous teaching and assessment. However, when students are held accountable for what they read, they cannot concentrate simply on the joy of reading. Gallo (1968) points out that young people have many reasons for reading, and the chief reason is for pleasure: "Without a doubt, most students read primarily for enjoyment, and a book ceases to be worth reading as soon as it ceases to be enjoyable" (535). Oliver (1976) reports that when there is an absence of any required performance level, it reduces the frustration of the attempts of learners to read more difficult books. He observes that the students in his free reading program felt confident to select more difficult books as the program progressed.

In terms of the usual kinds of accountability measures used to gauge reading comprehension, many advocates of free reading programs agree that book reports, log and notebook entries, comprehension questions, and oral retells are not recommended as assigned activities after the free reading periods. Such requirements send messages to students that teachers do not believe that they are really reading. Carlsen and Sherrill (1988) state that book reports do "more to kill young people's interest in reading than to promote it" and actually become "a source of irritation, ranging from mild to violent dislike" (154–155). They add that other activities that are despised by students include the literary notebook and oral presentations, even when the presentations are about books the students actually like. Suggesting that this may be, in part, because students become impatient and baffled by the search for meaning in a literacy work, these authors highlight the sense of anxiety and worthlessness students feel when their own responses to a piece of writing never seem to be enough.

For those of us who have witnessed students' excitement about books they have read, only to be followed by a sort of depression when they find out they have to do something "creative" with the book, this information is nothing new. When I first told my students about how we would do SSR, they were suspicious at best. They asked me several times whether I was being honest with them about not having book reports or journal entries. However, when I assured them that the point of SSR was simply to enjoy reading, they were thrilled. We can see that "even the able readers are relieved because they don't have to prove that they are bright every time they read something" (McCracken 1971, 582).

As adults, if we are honest with ourselves, we know that when we read something, we don't want to have to do anything specific with it when we finish. We might want to tell a friend about it, we might like to jot down some personal notes for ourselves, we might want to sit alone and laugh or cry, or we might not want to do anything. Usually, we want to read another book like it right away. The one we have just finished is forgotten in our rush to select another one. When I was on leave for an extended period of time due to surgery, I discovered an author whom I had not known about—but one whom I thoroughly enjoyed. Somewhat depressed because I could not be at work and desperately in need of diversion and entertainment, I zealously read every novel that Anne Rivers Siddons had ever written. I didn't stop until I realized that there were no more to read. Not once during that time did I ever have the urge to write a book report about one of those books or make journal entries in a log about my responses to what I had read. But I did tell many of my friends about the stories I was reading—and I'm sure I managed to entice a few of them to read something written by my new favorite author, as well.

A language arts consultant with whom I once worked shared a similar story with me. She told me of a presentation she had attended, where the speaker asked the group of adults, "When you have just finished a wonderful book, don't you automatically say to yourself, 'Gee, I'd love to do a diamante!'" The entire audience laughed because, of course, the thought of doing any kind of book project had not crossed their minds, even though they may have enjoyed the book very much.

Teachers often ask me what counts as an accountability measure and what doesn't. I always tell them that if their students perceive a post-SSR activity as a method of applying "teacher-imposed evaluative criteria" (Everett 1987, 4), then it is an accountability measure. Student views determine what is acceptable and what is not. If young people become excited about their reading and desire to share their books with peers, then they have a range of possible activity options open to then. These are the follow-up activities that I discuss in the next section.

Follow-up Activities

The definition of follow-up activities is crucial because follow-up activities must be carefully distinguished from accountability measures. Clary (1991) remarks that students should not have to share "every book in any way" (343). However, when learners do decide to share, they should have a variety of choices—from designing costumes to creating ads, art projects, drama, book talks, and read-aloud scripts. There is much agreement that interactive, or sharing, activities which follow free reading periods can be positive contributions to reading programs.

Opportunities to Share Once students have become accustomed to independent reading, the teacher should encourage responses from them. If the teachers themselves talk about what they have read and "share their delight" with students, pupils begin to do the same (McCracken 407). In a Maryland study, students requested two additions to their free reading program: more time to read and an opportunity to discuss their books with others who had read the same ones (Petre 1971). It has been suggested that this is because books produce intellectual constructs in the minds of readers which can be better understood and appreciated by the readers if they are externalized by talking with others (Carlsen and Sherrill 1988). When I allowed my students to have three minutes at the end of SSR to talk to people at their table about their books, they begged for more time, since not everyone got a turn. At first I thought these wily students were trying to distract me from getting on with our class lessons, but as I listened carefully, I could tell that they really were enjoying their discussions about books. They had called me on the issue of not including enough follow-up activity time.

Diana, a teacher in one middle school classroom in Burbank, California, offered students opportunities to do what she called "sixty-second reviews" of their books. Volunteers were asked to stand up and tell the class what was happening in their books. They did not have to wait until they had finished the books but instead gave in-progress highlights. She also allowed students three-to-five minutes once in awhile after SSR to" tell a friend" what was going on in their stories. These activities, she maintained, promoted a good deal of book sharing among the students that probably would not otherwise have occurred; and many students signed up on waiting lists to assure themselves of reading some of the "good" books that had been presented.

The need to share a good book is a strong one, and we should be aware that modeling "talk about books" will open up doors for students who are usually quite shy. After SSR, I usually told at least two or three students what was happening in the book I was currently reading. If I happened to be sitting at a table with several students, more often than not at least one of them would ask me questions about my book and tell me a little bit about theirs. Following a few of these sharing sessions, one student who had never volunteered to read anything aloud during regular class activities actually asked to read aloud a funny portion of his book to all of his tablemates after reading one particularly humorous section during SSR.

Opportunities to Collaborate Aside from opportunities to read and to share, creative activities can sometimes help to foster enthusiasm for reading (Moore, Jones, and Miller 1980). These activities can include the development of student-produced newspapers with "book recommendation" sections, book and author luncheons, student-produced stories and plays, and various other projects. Chambers (1996) suggests developing a short program of stories, poems, and prose passages that are compiled and read as a spoken anthology, either by one reader or a group of readers. He also recommends serializing a story over a few days, where one reader or a group of readers do a read-aloud of one part to their peers each day until the story is finished.

One of the most interesting follow-up ideas I have heard of comes from the classroom of Mary Jo Sherman (1996) who, along with her students, "rediscovered letter writing" (510). In a log book, students wrote a letter a week (on a rotating basis over a three-week period) about what they had been reading to one of three possible recipients: a friend, a family member, or the teacher. The recipients of the letters then wrote back on the opposite sides of the log sheets. In this way, students enjoyed authentic dialogues about their reading with people whose opinions they valued. Sherman notes that these kinds of reflections on books and the connections made between the books and other readings eventually "evolved into literate conversations" (510) as the year progressed. The success of these letters further supports the idea that students have a "need to talk about their reading" (Carlsen and Sherrill 1988, 88).

Another social activity which can serve as a follow-up to reading (and in this case, writing, as well) is the Author's Chair, where students can read aloud to classmates a story that they have written themselves. The story then becomes part of the class reading collection, and others may choose to read it later in pairs or on their own. One of my students, Artin, was a truly gifted artist, but he didn't feel that he had much ability as a writer. I asked him to draw a series of cartoon frames representing a story that he could create. Being a fan of fast cars (and Mustangs, in particular), he developed an eight-frame story about a man who kept missing his bus to work in the morning and who finally decided to purchase a new car (a Mustang, of course). Once the picture story was in place, I asked him to select a classmate to help him write the story part, which he did. Together, they came up with a fun and imaginative story that high school students could easily relate to—the fantasy of owning a sporty new car. They read the story aloud to the class and were enthusiastically applauded by their classmates. After that, we put a title page together in order to celebrate the author and illustrator and made copies for the classroom library. Often I would see students reading that story during SSR, and some of them even asked the author questions about it later, with suggestions for possible sequels. The students in our bungalow were proud to have student-created stories in the classroom collection—and I don't have to tell you how important it made the author and illustrator feel!

Peer Encouragement One of the advantages of doing follow-up activities is that students interact with others about books, a process which provides a form of group approval of reading. Peer encouragement, especially for adolescents, is often a very powerful motivating factor. School friends have a large impact on whether or not reading becomes socially acceptable. This kind of influence can be used positively to motivate reluctant readers to join the group (Sadoski 1980).

One of my senior boys, who had read almost nothing for pleasure before entering my class, was quite concerned about how he might appear to his buddies if he started reading chapter books. Instead, he decided that magazines were "cool enough," and he embarked on a reading binge of different types and titles. One of the highlights of the year was when he came to me with questions about how to subscribe to a magazine: he wanted to order his own personal subscription to *Gentleman's Quarterly* (GQ). I was so excited that I practically wrote the check for him.

Self-Selection of Activities Certainly, a key to providing good follow-up activities is student involvement in them. The more freedom the students have to develop their own ideas, the greater the degree of ownership and engagement they will have in the activities. Whenever possible, suggest activities to your students and let them choose—or better yet, have them come up with their own. Students know best how they would like to channel their enthusiasm. (Just be sure the choices are legal and approved by the administration at your school.) We simply need to remember that whatever activities are selected as follow-ups to SSR should offer opportunities for interaction with others and for creative extensions of ideas developed during reading—but they should never be required.

Distributed Time to Read

It has been pointed out that "a reader is not merely a person who *can* read but a person who does read" (Sadoski 1980, 155). Unless students are provided with time to read in school, such reading may not occur at all. Teenagers, in particular, have so many other demands made on their time—homework, home chores, community and church activities, sports events, social engagements, and just "socializing" in general—that it is not surprising that reading often comes at the bottom of their priority list.

We do a good job of making sure that children learn to read in school, but oftentimes the love of reading is not instilled in some of them. These are the students who can read, but who rarely do it. In the early grades we read aloud to children, we show them beautifully-colored picture books, and we help them memorize, illustrate, act out and read wonderful stories. The world of reading is magical for a young child. But, by the start of fourth grade, somehow students begin to see reading as work. It is no longer an entertaining activity but a school task accompanied by worksheets, comprehension questions, quizzes, and tests. The introduction of textbooks after the primary grades makes this perception even stronger for many students.

No one would suggest that school reading and its concomitant activities are inappropriate. But the real problem is that school reading represents the bulk of the reading that some students do—at least for the students who are not avid readers. In-school free reading offers them opportunities to regain the thrill of reading something for pure enjoyment and, more important, leads the way to more reading outside of school by offering accessible and stimulating materials that they can take with them.

When starting your own SSR program, it is generally recommended that you begin with a "realistic" amount of time (Mork 1972). Older students generally need some time to get into their books and immerse themselves properly. I started with ten minutes and found that students had just begun to settle into their reading, so I extended the SSR period (in a fifty-five minute class period) to twelve to fifteen minutes. Of course, as students grow to cherish their SSR time, they will beg you for longer sessions. Only you know best how to balance curricular demands with reading time, but once in awhile a longer or whole period of SSR is a wonderful treat.

I have to admit that one time several years ago during a fifth-period high school class I forgot to stop SSR altogether. I had planned various group lessons for the post-SSR class time, but somehow we all started reading quietly, and the time just slipped away. For fifty minutes we were engrossed in our books. Finally, one of my students looked at the clock and said, "Dr. Pilgreen, you forgot our lesson!" I said, "Yes, I did, and I'll make it up to you. But look what a wonderful time we've all had!" No one, including myself, had realized how much time was passing as we read. As a community, we had experienced the joy of reading. But more important, my students were very impressed with themselves; they didn't know that they could read for so long and stay engaged.

I would bet that many of the students in my fifth-period class took their books home with them the evening following that long SSR period. And I'm certain that some of them read a good deal more before bedtime. They were simply too involved in those books to let them go. The act of reading in school and then reading at home has a spiraling effect. Reading in class promotes reading at home, and as students read more, they become better readers. Better readers enjoy reading more and therefore do more of it. The goal of in-class reading is to involve students in this cycle so that "the habit of reading will become part of our students' lifestyles" (Sanacore 1992, 470).

If we are to hook students on reading, then frequent opportunities to read in school are critical. Daily sessions of SSR are the most effective because in order for reading to become habitual, it must be done on a regular and "distributed" basis. It cannot be done all at once (on a "massed time" basis) for longer periods of time and have the same impact. Though students will certainly benefit from reading some rather than not reading at all, they will be less likely to develop the habit if they do not read in school frequently. When a new teacher who had attended Krashen's presentation on free voluntary reading shared with me how excited she was to begin a free reading program in her high school ESL class, I was pleased for her and her students. However, when she told me that she had given her students a choice about when to do the reading—every day for twelve minutes or once a week for an hour—I realized that she had unknowingly offered them "distributed" versus "massed" time approaches. Of course, the students chose what they considered to be "free time," rather than free reading time on Fridays, and by the end of a couple of weeks, the young teacher was frustrated because the students weren't really engaged in their books.

Jim Trelease (1995) makes a convincing case for reading aloud to our children not only when they are young but also as they progress through the upper grades. His point is that having someone read aloud to students is highly motivational for them. They love to be read to; they aspire to read as well as the proficient reader does; and they become interested in reading more. He also maintains that educators are doing just as good a job of teaching reading as we ever did—but that we, as a nation, have stopped reading aloud to our kids and have created a generation of readers who *can* read—but *don't* read. In the same way, aside from not reading aloud enough to our children, we often do not offer them the one gift they need to become lifelong readers—frequent time to do pleasure reading in school. Only by providing quality SSR programs can we truly attain the goal of creating readers who both *can* and *do* read. In Chapter 6, I suggest a wide array of resources that are available to help you reach this objective.

6

Problems, Perspectives, and Places to Go

As you develop your SSR program, you will discover the specific publishing companies that carry your students' favorite titles, the resources you'll need to organize book fairs and buy posters for your classroom, the book clubs that offer low-cost materials to enhance your classroom bookshelves and your students' personal libraries, and the organizations that can support you in your selection of materials. You'll also identify problems you hadn't anticipated, but they are all solvable, and they pale in comparison to the joy of helping students discover that they really like to read.

The remainder of this book is devoted to giving you an overview of (1) some of the implementational issues you may face; (2) the kinds of positive responses your might expect from your students after their participation in an effective SSR program; (3) the periodicals, comic books, series books, book clubs, and read-along books and tapes that are available; and (4) phone numbers and addresses of publishing companies and major organizations that can assist you.

Problems: Most Frequently Asked Questions

At conferences and workshops, teachers often share the problems related to SSR program implementation. The following represent some of the most frequently asked questions I receive—and the answers I give!

About Access

Q: My students seem to enjoy SSR time, but many of them take their books home for the evening and then forget to bring them back the next day for SSR! They tell me that they don't want to start anything new because they're already in the middle of a book they like. What should I do?

A: I recommend keeping a set of anthologies containing very short stories near your desk. My students could read a whole story in one SSR period and then go back to reading the book they'd already started. New magazines, comics, cartoon books, and joke books are also good one-period intrigues.

However, if forgetting books becomes a trend, it means that the books are not the right matches for the students in the first place; otherwise, bringing them to class would be a priority for them. You might need to find out more about what would suit these readers' interests.

Q: A big problem that I face is that the students want to keep getting out of their seats to find books from the bookshelves during SSR. This often leads to lots of socializing and very little reading. What can I do to be sure there is a minimum of activity during this quiet time—but still let them change books when they need to?

A: While we do want students to be able to change books if they don't like what they're reading, we also want our SSR environments to be peaceful. I solved the problem by allowing students who needed to find new books to take four or five books to their desks during SSR. They could spend the whole period browsing through these "possibles" in order to choose something they felt they would enjoy. I advised them to read two or three pages from each book to get a sense of the author's style, the reading level, and the story line or content.

If I noticed that the students checked out something at the end of the SSR period, I didn't become further involved. However, if they weren't successful in finding interesting reading, I would usually ask them to drop by after school, during snack, or at the end of lunch in order to chat about what they might like. (Sometimes I even wrote notes with offers to help.)

Just a word of warning, though; you might want to keep your eye on the books when students have several at one time. Gail, a middle school teacher from Upland couldn't find some of her more popular classroom books and finally located them in one student's desk. Jason, the young man, had been hoarding about ten of the "good books" for his own SSR pleasure!

Q: I've been trying to build up my SSR classroom library, and I've spent a lot of money (both the school's and my own) on the materials. Yet, I lost more than $100 worth of books last year. What can I do to ensure that students return them?

A: You need to set up a practical record-keeping system that places some responsibility on the readers and helps you to keep track of your materials. Marj, a teacher at Glendale High School, asks her instructional assistants to help. Whenever a student wants to take a book home, he fills out a library card and gives it to the assistant, who files it under the student's name in a file box.

When he returns the book, the assistant crosses off his name and places the card in the book pocket of the book, to be returned to the classroom shelf.

Middle school and high school students can also serve as SSR librarians if you don't have another adult in the classroom. On a rotating basis, they can operate as the "librarian of the week." Many students enjoy being given responsible positions in your classroom and feel proud of their roles as leaders in the class SSR program.

Q: We have a great school library, and I feel lucky that we can send students to check out books during any class period. However, I have one or two students who ask to go to the library several times a week during SSR to find new books. Should I just tell them they can't go anymore? I give them passes quite often, but they don't seem to come back with books they can stick with for any period of time.

A: As we know, sometimes students don't always level with us about their reasons for what they do! When students ask for library passes too often, you can call ahead and hook the students up to the librarian to help. If they're simply wanting time to socialize, the visits will stop once they receive the extra adult help. But if they really need help, they'll get it!

I think it's important to allow students to use the school library during SSR, as long as they don't take undue advantage of the outside-of-class freedom. I used to offer students a couple of library passes every two weeks. Most kids didn't want to go if they had books they liked, but some found it enjoyable to see what was available in addition to our classroom collection. Of course, we should remind them to visit the library during lunch, snack, and after school, as well. During these times, they have more opportunity to browse without having to be back in class right away.

About Appeal

Q: Even though we've been offering free reading time in class since September and it's almost Thanksgiving, some of my students still have a hard time buying into the concept of SSR. However, I've been asking them to read books. I know that students are usually allowed to read other materials during SSR, but I'm not sure how comfortable I feel about letting students read magazines and newspapers. Will they really read them?

A: I know this is a tough issue for many teachers, but sometimes periodicals are the only materials that will engage reluctant readers at first. Students often associate "books" with school—and magazines and newspapers with real life. One teacher told me that she had a student who brought *Auto Mechanic* books to school and was amazed to find out that he was encouraged to use them for SSR. As she put it, he said he "didn't know he was reading" as he spent hours poring over them.

One study in Columbia, Missouri, focused on the impact of light reading materials on junior high school students' library use and reading patterns (Dorrell and Carroll 1981). Library traffic experienced an "immediate and lasting change" after the introduction of comic books into the school library (18). According to the researchers, the comics signaled students that there was something in the library for them—and that the library was open and comfortable.

It's important to help students start viewing reading as an enjoyable activity and not simply a school task. A logical first step is to offer periodicals that relate directly to their outside-of- school interests. Getting them involved in reading in the first place is the critical issue, and light reading may provide the necessary motivation.

Q: I love the idea of students selecting their own books to read! However, I sometimes worry about some of the books they bring from home or from their friends' collections. I'm concerned that parents will call the principal and complain, especially about some of the material that is kind of violent or too "mature."

A: It's true that not everything our students choose would be considered appropriate by parents, and some materials will actually have to be banned from the classroom (such as adult magazines that are sold in "specialty shops"—or anything else that would lead to your dismissal as a teacher)! However, if specific books are questionable, I usually ask students to have their parents sign permission slips allowing them to read the books.

It's also a good idea to get together with other teachers who provide SSR time in their classes, as well as with your school administrators, and discuss what materials you consider inappropriate for classroom use. Then, keep these guidelines in mind when you add to your SSR collections and communicate with parents.

Q: When we first started doing SSR, I didn't allow my students to read magazines, but then I was given some school money for subscriptions, and I relented. Now I find that while they are very popular sources, many students spend a lot of time just looking at the pictures. Do you have any suggestions for how to deal with this?

A: No one could argue that the pictures in magazines aren't part of what make them appealing! But students can spend a great deal of time simply looking at them and not reading. I had discussions with my high school students about how reading improves all of their language skills, and I teased them that looking at pictures would only make them better at looking at pictures. We agreed, though, that the fun part of a new classroom magazine was first looking at the pictures, so I told them that one SSR period of just browsing through a magazine to see what articles it included and what pictures it contained would be acceptable. Then I asked them to choose an article that interested them to read for the following day. They thought this was a fair procedure and almost always volunteered their choices to me by the end of the browsing period.

About Conducive Environments

Q: I understand that students don't necessarily have to sit in neat, tidy rows during SSR, but it's difficult for me to think of letting them read stretched out on the floor, in pillow chairs, or crowded together on a classroom sofa. I wouldn't feel I'd have any control over the amount of socializing that would occur.

A: There are many ways to make the seating more comfortable (and the environment more relaxing) during SSR if you are anxious about having students out of their seats. Students can sit at circular tables, or in grouped arrangements composed of regular desks, where they feel a stronger sense of classroom community. You can also allow them to sit with friends of their choice during the free reading time, with the understanding that the "quiet rule" still prevails. The most important aspect of a conducive environment is that students are given uninterrupted time to read in comfortable surroundings and that there is a pervasive feeling among the students that this time is both enjoyable and "sacred."

Q: This may seem like a strange problem, but I sometimes have students in class who literally cannot sit still for the whole SSR time. They fidget, tap their feet, and just generally annoy everyone around them. What do you do about students who can't pay attention or who need to move around?

A: This is not an unusual question, but my answer may seem unconventional. Some students need a more flexible seating arrangement or the opportunity to move around a bit while they are reading. Jessica, a teacher at Claremont High School, had a student who couldn't sit still, but he did like to read. She allowed him to wander in the back of the classroom while he did his reading for SSR. He didn't socialize with anyone and stayed glued to his book—while he was pacing back and forth! Of course, your ability to be this flexible will depend on your tolerance levels and whether your class is distracted by the movement or not. But there's no rule that says SSR must be stationary, only sustained and silent!

About Encouragement

Q: I was very excited when I started offering students time to read during class because *I* learned to read by getting involved in series books (*The Happy Hollisters* and the *Bobbsey Twins*, in particular). Now I'm concerned when I see some of them sticking to the same series month after month when the books seem too easy for them. Will their reading improve by doing this?

A: Yes, eventually, but you have to be patient and secure in the knowledge that you are doing the right thing by continuing to let students self-select their own reading choices. Sometimes it takes a period of time for students to exhaust their interest in a particular series, but it will happen. When Yolanda, a tenth grader, started reading the *Sweet Valley High* series, I thought she'd never put the books down. But she kept reading diligently and was always so immersed in her books that she sometimes hid them in her lap and tried to read them after SSR during the group lesson. At the end of her tenth grade year, she asked me where she could find another romance writer who was more sophisticated. Though she stayed with the romance genre, she then graduated to reading Danielle Steel books, which have a higher reading level. I also introduced her to some fantasy books that included an element of romance but helped her extend into a new genre.

    I had a similar experience with my own daughter, who recently bought *Sense and Sensibility* and *Emma* by Jane Austen. When she was fourteen, she read every series book written by Young Adult author Lurlene McDaniels. Now that she's sixteen, she's reading everything Jane Austen ever wrote! If she hadn't started reading avidly when she was younger, she would not be such a proficient reader of the classics now!

Q: My classes have been doing SSR for awhile, but I would still like to see the students view themselves more keenly as readers—or members of what Frank Smith calls "The Literacy Club." How can I help them do this?

A: There are many ways to help students feel a part of the club, and having students engage in SSR on a regular basis is the primary one. However, a teacher named Joyce told me about some girls in her Marantha High School class in Sierra Madre who stood in front of the class bookshelf at the end of the school year and pointed to all the books they had read. They were so proud of themselves! We can help students have this sense of accomplishment by asking them to keep a list of the books they've read during the school year in a folder or portfolio. When they see the list growing (and the reading material usually getting harder), they have no questions about their membership in the club! (See Appendix N for an example of a School Year Reading Log.)

Norma, a teacher in the Azusa Unified School District, highlighted the Literacy Club idea in a different way: by organizing a Breakfast Reading Club, which met before school once a week to discuss the books the students had read. The students in that group certainly identified themselves as readers!

Q: I've told my ESL students that reading during SSR will help them to read better, but they don't really believe me. They seem to think that they're not really "doing anything" when they're just reading. How can I help them understand how important it is?

A: Terri, a teacher at Northview Intermediate in the Duarte Unified School District, said that her students wouldn't take it seriously either until she made a concerted effort to explain all of the benefits of SSR and to read each day with them. She resisted phone calls, paper grading, and other interruptions and they got the message that SSR was "sacred." She also told them stories about what she used to read when she was a child—and they settled down considerably. They wanted to be just like her.

Q: When I first started having independent reading time in my classes, I had great hopes that within a couple of weeks, everyone in my class would have found books they liked and be happily reading! But I noticed that some kids grabbed a new book every day and never finished it. How much time does it take for SSR to "catch on"?

A: Marina, a high school ESL teacher in the Glendale Unified School District, would tell you that it takes longer for some students to become involved than others—but it will happen! One of her students couldn't find the right book for six months. When he found *Hatchet* by Gary Paulsen, he developed overnight from a non-reader into a reader! Now he reads all the time! She has shared this success story with her colleagues in the hopes of spreading the word that sometimes patience is the best form of encouragement.

Von Sprecken and Krashen (1998) observed eleven language-arts classes during SSR time at the middle school level. Results showed that by the middle of the year, ninety percent of the students were reading during SSR time!

Q: Even though I always talk to my students about how wonderful reading is, I still haven't heard rave reviews from them about having SSR time in my class. Am I asking for too much to want to see some display of enthusiasm?

A: Maybe so. After all, students who like to read and students who *say* they like to read are two different things. We have to remember that permission to see reading as "cool" has to come from the students themselves. Joyce, a teacher at Crescenta Valley High School, noted that her students would never actually say that they liked SSR—but when a fire drill or other unplanned activity took away their time to read, they were upset.

Q: I think SSR is a great idea for students in regular classes, but I'm not sure my Special Education students would really buy into it. They love to have me read with them, and sometimes they take turns reading aloud, but I'm not sure they could actually read quietly on their own for the whole SSR time. Isn't the main issue whether they read or not? Does it matter if we all read the same book together or whether they read their own books?

It's true that sharing a good book is a wonderful experience, but if we want students to become lifelong readers, they need to be able to read—and want to read—on their own. Ann, a teacher at Upland Junior High School, taught Resource classes and decided to start an SSR program for her students. She was thrilled when, for the first time, they starting asking her if they could check out books to read at home!

About Staff Training

Q: At our school, some teachers think SSR is great, while others think it has no place in a secondary school. Our principal was considering having an SSR time each day when everyone in the whole school would stop and read. I'm in favor of SSR, but I'm not sure the whole staff would truly support it.

A: You have just raised two critical issues: staff buy-in and access to books. If the people involved with SSR don't subscribe to the philosophy underlying it, the SSR program may be doomed before it starts. Asking everyone to participate without being sure that they believe in its benefits will lead to non-participation and sabotage on the part of the nay-sayers. Students will know that the adults are not taking it seriously and will follow suit. Also, before any schoolwide SSR program can be implemented, reading materials must be available whenever students are asked to read—which typically means in all classes at the same time each day. It's difficult to provide a degree of comfort and a wide variety of reading materials in a P.E. class; a language lab; or a science classroom with sinks, stools, and bunsen burners. Sometimes secondary schools have more success offering SSR only in the classrooms where teachers who are committed to its philosophy are willing to put in the effort to address all of the eight factors.

Q: We tried doing SSR at our middle school and found that some of the teachers who didn't want to do it were letting students have free time instead of reading. Is there any way to encourage these teachers to join the effort?

A: One school where I consulted asked the very same question, and they decided that if they couldn't get full support from all staff members, they would offer SSR in their English and ESL classes, where teachers were committed to it— and then request support from the other content-area teachers. Teachers who weren't offering SSR were asked to encourage students in their independent reading efforts by asking them questions about their independent reading, discussing the books and topics they were interested in, and sharing their own reading habits and preferences with the students. Instead of undermining the SSR effort, the content-area teachers were then able to provide a measure of support for the program.

About Accountability

Q: I know I'm not supposed to make students accountable for what they read (or how much they read) during SSR, but at the beginning of each school year, I have some students who simply won't focus on reading, especially if they've never had SSR opportunities in class before. Is there any way to give them some kind of credit for reading?

A: I've agonized over this issue myself, keeping in mind that anything the students view as an accountability measure *is* an accountability measure. However, I did find that giving students credit simply for the act of participating in SSR (rather than for how many pages or books they read or how much they understood) was helpful when I first began SSR with a new class. I stamped students' Reading Records (see Appendix H), indicating that they had shared in the SSR process "silently and in a sustained way." If they wished to add responses to their reading, they could also do so (on an optional basis) as preparation for a short table discussion of their reading.

However, while some students enjoyed the closure the Reading Record provided (and relied upon it to tell them what page they should start on each time they returned to the book), others tired of it and simply wanted to read without having to write down anything. (My observation was that for the students who were not habitual readers, the records provided a tangible way for them to see themselves as Literacy Club members.) You can judge the student response over several weeks and then eliminate (or make optional) the Reading Record if you feel it's not a positive component.

About Follow-up Activities

Q: It's so hard to provide time to read in class *plus* follow-up activities to give students time to respond to what they have read! What do busy teachers do when they want to provide SSR time but need to cover the curricular content, too?

A: You're absolutely right, so you may find avenues for student response that don't take a great deal of your class time. Many of the comic book companies now have Web sites where readers can log on to say how they felt about the latest issue, and some of these responses are printed in the next issues in the

Figure 6–1. A tenth grader shows her teacher the newest book title listed on her Reading Record.

form of the reader's e-messages! (For example, in *Batman*, it's called "Bat Signals.") Students can do this kind of follow-up activity at home and then briefly report on the activity to their classmates. Similarly, some book publishers ask students to write letters telling them whether or not they enjoyed the book. These are interactive, fun, and authentic activities that students can do outside of class—and then discuss with their classmates when you do have some time set aside for sharing.

I would also encourage you to offer follow-up activities that take a minimum amount of class time but do provide the much-needed outlet students need to share their excitement about reading. Diana, a teacher at Luther Burbank Middle School in Burbank, has three-minute book reviews in her classes, which one student per day volunteers to give after SSR. The students love hearing them because they give a thumb-nail sketch of possible new titles to read, and they don't take much time away from the fifty-five-minute class periods.

About Distributed Time to Read

Q: I've always thought that giving students time in class to read was important, but I'd rather offer whole chunks of time (e.g., during assembly days, on Fridays, etc.) than using much-needed class time each day which detracts from our curriculum.

A: The tendency *is* to want to not "waste" class time, but I encourage you to think about offering SSR time as an important educational component of your class curriculum. If you can get students to become involved in the habit of reading (which happens only if they read daily—not during infrequent chunks of time), you can lead them to become lifelong readers and learners. Equally important, if you offer appealing reading materials that relate to your content area, you help them develop background knowledge and interest in the subject you are teaching—and they'll better understand the content of your lessons because it will be more comprehensible. Then, the fifteen minutes a day that you devote to reading can be considered time well-spent rather than time used up.

Figure 6–2. Stephanie gears up to do a three-minute book review after SSR.

Perspectives: High School ESL Students' Responses to SSR

At the end of the first semester of the school year (which marked the conclusion of the full-fledged SSR study), we asked our ESL students to tell us their thoughts about their SSR experiences during the fall and to share their SSR "reading plans" for the spring. I'd like to highlight some of their comments because they led me to recognize just how important SSR was in terms of helping students to develop the habit—and spread the joy—of reading.

Anna (Tenth Grader):

Some of the kinds of things I read during the first semester were short stories and books. I took my book home and finished them because I couldn't wait to see what was going to happen.

Jaime (Eleventh Grader):

It was fun to have fifteen minutes of time to read. This semester I am planning to read long stories and more books than I read in first semester. My favorite author is Christopher Pike. I was interested in the series of Final Friends. It had three books: *The Party*, *The Dance*, and *The Graduation*.

Sun Sook (Tenth Grader):

My Developmental Reading class was the only class I had where I could read things for fun. I have read the novel called *White Fang* written by Jack London, and I even took it home so that I could read it more at home. However, if I wouldn't have had the SSR period, I wouldn't have read anything at home.

Maria (Twelfth Grader):

Now the new semester is starting, I feel the fifteen minutes of SSR each day is good for me because I can have a little time to read in class. It warms up our brains. My vocabulary is better, and I have noticed that my understanding of English has improved.

Esther (Eleventh Grader):

Even though I would start the books in class, I would take them home and finish because I couldn't wait to see what happened at the end.

Tony (Tenth Grader):

When I first came to the Developmental of Reading class, I felt kind of weird about the SSR. At first it was hard for me to read without talking, but then I got used to it.

Marieta (Eleventh Grader):

It didn't matter to me how long we read because once I got into reading I didn't know how fast time passes.

Narine (Eleventh Grader):

I plan on doing at least half an hour of reading at home each day before sleeping. My vocabulary has changed a lot and also my everyday words that I use.

Rory (Twelfth Grader):

The most wonderful thing in this class is that we actually get time to read individually the stuff that we prefer.

Thu (Tenth Grader):

I like to read adventure, fiction, or comedy books. During the first semester I was hooked on fiction books. When I began reading, I didn't want to stop, even for a minute. Now I want to read the harder books.

Armine (Tenth Grader):

I have developed some favorite authors after I have read many books. Two of my favorite authors are Anne Schraff and James Patterson. These two authors have a lot of books about the mysterious and murder story.

Chris (Eleventh Grader):

Now that the new semester is starting, I feel that fifteen minutes of SSR time is not enough for me. I started to like small articles like jokes, short stories, love stories, and others, and I am also planning to read twenty-five to thirty minutes at home every day.

Artie (Tenth Grader):

During second semester of SSR I would like to learn more about American authors and more about the "world" that is hidden inside of each book!

Ara (Tenth Grader):

I have become interested in the sports and comedy during SSR, and I want to subscribe for the *Sports Illustrated*.

Lucretia (Eleventh Grader):

I like a lot when you allowed us to read newspapers and magazines because I could get information about modern things.

Christina (Twelfth Grader):

I really liked SSR period we had because it really gave me the great opportunity to read in a silence and understand what I read.

Rosa (Eleventh Grader):

The things I read now are harder than the things I read in September because I can read now a lot faster and understand more.

Artur (Twelfth Grader):

I like reading books that were written from a live experience. It makes the book more interesting and encourages me to read more. Reading a lot makes me learn more, and it also makes my learning abilities to become more intelligent and smart. I pick out books that are hard to read. I always choose books that are very thick because it makes me feel that I can do it, and I can.

Marina (Eleventh Grader):

Now I am planning to read romantic books. I am interested in reading a romantic book called *P.S. I Love You*. The books are getting harder and longer now than before because I used to read short easy books.

Jordan (Tenth Grader):

I feel good about SSR because it makes me forget about other things and relax. I plan to read books and magazines about sports and mysteries.

Sung (Tenth Grader):

I wish we could read in class two times a week for twenty-five minutes, and the other three days for fifteen minutes. I like the idea of silent reading every day. My favorite author is Nancy Norton. She writes books about teenagers and how life is for them.

Gevorg (Eleventh Grader):

I always have two books—one of them I read it at home and the other one during SSR. But if I really liked my book and it came up to the main point, I took it home and finished it.

Geoffrey (Twelfth Grader):

I really liked the SSR because I got a little time to settle down with a good book. In that time, I got a chance to read *Jurassic Park* and other books. Sometimes when I read I get excited, and I don't want to stop reading so I take the book home.

Gagik (Tenth Grader):

I plan to read magazines because I like the pictures, because it makes it interesting for me, and I like it because there are lots of different things that I like to read in it, especially football and hunting.

Henrietta (Eleventh Grader):

It would be better to have more time for SSR because like yesterday I was really interested in it, but it was not enough time to read.

Brian (Tenth Grader):

I like to read because you can be anywhere in a book.

Cecilia (Tenth Grader):

And so many thanks to you, dear teacher, for letting us to read during SSR because we love it so much.

Final Reflections

As you might expect, we continued our SSR program throughout the remainder of the school year—and our students stayed highly engaged and positive. Many of them went into regular English classes the following year, but they dropped by often to tell us how much they missed the reading class and what they were reading. Often, they even checked out books from us. I know that our students continued reading as they progressed through higher grade levels and into college because they came back to visit and told us! Recently, I returned to my old bungalow at the Home School, and I chatted with Albert, one of my wonderful instructional aides who participated in the "spirit of reading" with our ESL students during the study. He handed me a box that one of our ex-students had brought to school to give to me. In it was a necklace from Raymond, the young man who had hated to read aloud but stayed in our class for three years, and who is now in college. The card read, "To Dr. Pilgreen, to thank you for everything." He asked Albert to tell me that he is reading all of the John Grisham books.

Places to Go: Resources for SSR Programs

As you develop or seek to enhance your SSR program, consider some of the following resources for books, magazines, and reading-related materials, such as posters and book marks for your classroom. (Where publishing companies' addresses and telephone numbers are listed, please note that while I tried to locate current information, it often changes quickly.) I would recommend keeping a file box or phone book with publishing company information, phone numbers, and local representatives' names. (Many companies offer 800 numbers, which is a real advantage when you need to do a great deal of calling.) That way, if you need to ask questions or buy more materials, the information is at your fingertips!

Support Organizations

American Library Association
50 E. Huron Street
Chicago, Illinois 60611
(312) 944-6780
(800) 545-2433
http://www.ala.org

For orders:
155 N. Wacker Drive
Chicago, Illinois 60606
http://www.alastore.ala.org

The American Library Association (ALA) has many publications which offer book lists and award-winning titles. One book that is a "must have" is *ALA's Guide to Best Reading* (updated yearly), which has a large section devoted to Young Adult Literature, including "Best Books for Young Adults" and "Popular Paperbacks for Young Adults." It contains reproducible, loose-leaf lists that can be folded into pamphlets and distributed freely on an unlimited basis.

You can also subscribe to *Book Links*, a periodical which connects books, libraries, and classrooms by providing reviews and annotated bibliographies of new books for readers of all ages.

The ALA Graphics Catalog, *READ*, published several times a year, includes posters, bookmarks, and other reading-related items which can boost motivation for reading in your classroom.

International Reading Association
800 Barksdale Road
PO Box 8139
Newark, DE 19714-8139
(302) 731-1600

(800) 336-READ
http://www.reading.org

The International Reading Association (IRA) publishes *Teens' Favorite Books: Young Adults' Choices, More Teens' Favorite Books: Young Adults' Choices,* and *Magazines for Kids and Teens,* as well as many other articles and lists of popular titles related to young adult interests in the *Journal of Adolescent and Adult Literacy.*

National Council of Teachers of English
1111 W. Kenyon Road
Urbana, Illinois 61801-1096
(217) 328-3870
(800) 369-6283
fax (217) 328-3870
http://www.ncte.org

The National Council of Teachers of English (NCTE) offers a variety of publications related to adolescent reading interests: *Speaking for Ourselves* (Autobiographical Sketches by Notable Authors of Young Adults), *Literature for Teenagers, A Jar of Tiny Stars* (Poems by NCTE Award-Winning Poets), *Books for You* (An Annotated Booklist for Senior High), *Your Reading* (An Annotated Booklist for Middle School and Junior High), and *High Interest—Easy Reading* (An Annotated Booklist for Middle School and Senior High School, seventh Edition). NCTE also publishes the journals *Voices from the Middle* for middle school and junior high school teachers and the *English Journal* for high school teachers, both of which provide information on young adult literature.

Book Clubs for Older Readers

TAB: The Teen Book Club
Scholastic Book Clubs, Inc.
Jefferson City, Missouri 65102-7503
(800) 724-6527
http://www.scholastic.com/tab
(Book Fairs available)

Troll 6–9 Book Club
Troll Book Clubs
2 Lethbridge Plaza
Mahwah, New Jersey 07430
(800) 541-1097
http://www.troll.com
(Book Fairs available)

TRUMPET 4–6 (Easier Reading)
   The Trumpet Club
   P.O. Box 7510
   Jefferson City, Missouri 65102-7510
   (800) 826-0110

Classroom Magazine Subscriptions

   Published by Scholastic, Inc:
   Scholastic Action (Grades 7–12, Reading Levels 3–5)
   Scholastic Scope: Language Arts (Grades 7–12)
   Science World (Grades 7–10)
   Junior Scholastic (Grades 6–8)
   Scholastic Math (Grades 6–9)
   Scholastic Art (Grades 7–12)
   Literary Cavalcade (Grades 9–12)
   Scholastic Update: Social Studies (Grades 9–12)
   Scholastic Choices: Family and Consumer Science/Health (Grades 7–12)
Current Events (Published by the Weekly Reader Corporation): News articles for middle grade students, written at lower readability levels.
National Geographic Adventure (Published by the National Geographic Society): Articles about adventurous people, suitable for young adults.
National Geographic World (Published by the National Geographic Society): Articles for younger readers, through middle school ages.
News for You (Published by New Reader's Press): Weekly editions of rewrites of news articles, written for teenagers at a fourth-sixth grade reading level.

Favorite Magazines for Young Adults

Celebrities
- Teen People
- People
- Hit Parades
- Movieline
- Biography
- Entertainment Weekly

Sports/Outdoor Activities
- Sports Illustrated for Kids
- Sports Illustrated
- Climbing
- Bicycling
- Cycle Sport

- Outdoor Life
- Skin Diver
- Wind Surfing
- Snowboarder
- Sport Fishing
- Soccer

News
- Newsweek
- Time

Fashion/Glamour
- Jane
- Teen
- YM
- Twist
- American Girl
- Seventeen
- InStyle
- Jump

Music
- Bass
- Player
- Guitar
- New Music
- Modern Drum
- Keyboard

Cars and Bikes
- Hot Rod
- Sport Rider
- Hot Bike
- Corvette Fever
- Autosport
- Motocross Action

Comic Books

Archie Comic Publications, Inc.
325 Fayette Avenue
Mamaroneck, New York 10543-2318
http://www.archiecomics.com

Titles such as:
- Archie
- Cheryl and Blossom
- Sabrina the Teenage Witch
- Betty
- Veronica
- Archie's Pal, Jughead

Marvel Comics
A Division of Marvel Enterprises, Inc.
Office of Publication
387 Park Avenue South
New York, New York 10016
http://www.marvel.com

Titles such as:
- Captain America
- Slingers
- Webspinners: Tales of Spiderman
- CABLE
- Gambit
- The Invincible Iron Man
- The Avengers
- Fantastic Four
- X-Force

D.C. Comics
1700 Broadway
New York, New York 10019

Subscriptions:
D.C. Comics Subscriptions
P.O. Box 0528
Baldwin, New York 11510
http://www.Dccomics.com
Keyword: DC comics on AOL

Titles such as:
- Batman
- Nightwing
- The Adventures of Superman
- Justice League of America

- Robin
- Animaniacs
- The Flintstones
- The Jetsons

Dark Horse Comics, Inc.
10956 SE Main Street
Milwaukie, Oregon 97222

Titles such as:
- Star Wars Episode I

Bongo Entertainment, Inc.
1440 S. Sepulveda Blvd., 3rd Floor
Los Angeles, California 90025
(310) 966-6168

Titles such as:
- Simpsons Comics

Romance and Daily Life (An asterisk in the following series book sections represents a readability level below sixth grade—easier reading)

Love Stories by various authors (Bantam Double Day Dell)
Titles such as *Stolen Kisses* by Liesa Abrams, *While You Were Gone* by Kieran Scott, and *Trust Me* by Kieran Scott

Sweet Valley High by Francine Pascal (Bantam Double Day Dell)
Titles such as *What Jessica Wants, Fight Fire with Fire,* and *Elizabeth is Mine*

Sweet Valley University by Francine Pascal (Bantam Double Day Dell)
Titles such as *College Girls* and *Anything for Love*

Roswell High Series by Melinda Metz (Pocket Books)
Titles such as *The Outsider, The Wild One,* and *The Watcher*

Clearwater Crossing Series by Laura Peyton Roberts (Bantam Double Day Dell)
Titles such as *Heart and Soul; Get a Life; Reality Check;* and *Promises, Promises*

Heart Beats by Elizabeth M. Rees (Aladdin Paperbacks)
Titles such as *Moving As One, Body Lines, Latin Nights,* and *Last Dance*

The Year I Turned Sixteen Series by Diane Schwemm (Pocket Books)
Titles such as *Rose, Daisy, Laurel,* and *Lily*

Life at Sixteen Series by Cheryl Lanham (Berkley Books)
Titles such as *Blue Moon, Second Best,* and *No Guarantees*

Leaving Home: On the Road Series by Stephanie Doyon (Simon and Schuster)
Titles such as *Leaving Home, Buying Time, Taking Chances,* and *Making Waves*

Dawson's Creek Series by various authors (Pocket Books)
Titles such as *Double Exposure* by C. J. Anders, *Major Meltdown* by K. S. Rodrigues, and *Calm Before the Storm* by Jennifer Baker

Clueless Series by various authors (Pocket Books)
Titles such as *Southern Fried Makeover* by Carla Jablonski, *Extreme Sisterhood* by Randi Reisfeld, and *Friend or Faux* by H. B. Gilmour

College Life 101 Series by Wendy Corsi Staub (Berkley Books)
Titles such as *Kim: The Party, Camerson: The Sorority,* and *Allison: The Townie*

One Last Wish Series by Lurlene McDaniels (Bantam Double Day Dell)
Titles Such as *A Time to Die, Mourning Song,* and *Let Him Live*

*Silverleaf Series by Anne Schraff (Perfection Learning Corporation)
Titles such as *Web of the Spider, Mister Fudge* and *Missy Moran, The Whispering Shell,* and *The Vampire Bat Girls' Club*

*Passages Series by Anne Schraff (Perfection Learning Corporation)
Titles such as *An Alien Spring, Don't Blame the Children, Please Don't Ask Me to Love You,* and *Shadow Man*

Historical and Historical Fiction

Anne of Green Gables by L. M. Montgomery (HarperCollins Publishers)
Titles such as *Anne of Green Gables, Anne of Avonlea,* and *Anne of the Island*

*My Name is America Series by various authors (Scholastic, Inc.)
Titles such as *The Journal of William Thomas Emerson: A Revolutionary War Patriot* by Barry Denenberg; *The Journal of James Edmond Pease: A Civil War Union Soldier* by Jim Murphy; and *The Journal of Joshua Loper* by Walter Dean Myers

*Dear America Series by various authors (Scholastic, Inc.)
Titles such as *The Winter of Red Snow: The Revolutionary War Diary of Abigail Jane Stewart* by Kristiana Gregory; *Voyage on the Great Titanic: The Diary of Margaret Ann Brady* by Ellen Emerson White; and *A Journey to the New World: The Diary of Remember Patience Whipple* by Kathryn Lasky

*Childhood of Famous Americans (Aladdin Paperbacks)
Titles such as *Susan B. Anthony, Daniel Boone, Albert Einstein, Harry Houdini, John F. Kennedy, Martin Luther King, Jr.,* and *Jim Thorpe*

Science Fiction

Tripods Trilogy by John Christopher (Aladdin Paperbacks)
Titles such as *White Man, When the Tripods Came, Pool of Fire,* and the *City of Gold and Lead*

Star Trek: The Next Generation by various authors (Simon and Schuster)
Titles such as *Ship of the Line* by Diane Carey

Star Trek: Deep Space Nine by various authors (Simon and Schuster)
Titles such as *The 34th Rule* by Armin Shimerman and David R. George III, *Rebels* by Daffyd ab Hugh, and *What You Leave Behind* by Diane Carey

Star Wars: Galaxy of Fears by John Whitman (Bantam Double Day Dell)
Titles such as *Army of Terror; Clones,* and *Eaten Alive*

Adventure and Fantasy

Chronicles of Narnia by C. S. Lewis (HarperCollins Publishers)
Titles such as *Prince Caspian, Magician's Nephew, Horse and His Boy,* and *Silver Chair*

World of Adventure Series by Gary Paulsen (Bantam Double Day Dell)
Titles such as *The Rock Jockeys, Captive,* and *Time Bender*

The X-Files by Eric Elfman (HarperCollins Publishers)
Titles such as *Our Town, The Calusari,* and *Hungry Ghosts*

Song of the Lioness Quartet by Tamora Pierce (Random House, Inc.)
Titles such as *Alanna, The First Adventure, In the Hand of The Goddess, The Woman Who Rides Like a Man,* and *Lioness Rampant*

Watchers Series by Peter Larangis (Scholastic, Inc.)
Titles such as *Rewind, Last Stop,* and *War*

Mystery and Detective

Net Force Series by Tom Clancy (Berkley Books)
Titles such as *One is the Loneliest Number, The Ultimate Escape,* and *Virtual Vandals*

Mystery Series by Philip Pullman (Random House, Inc.)
Titles such as *Broker Bridge, Shadow in the North,* the *Tin Princess,* and *The White Mercedes*

The Dark Materials Series by Philip Pullman (Random House, Inc.)
Titles such as *The Golden Compass* and *The Subtle Knife*

The Hardy Boys Casefiles by Franklin W. Dixon (Pocket Books)
Titles such as *Beyond the Law, Spiked,* and *Open Season*

The Nancy Drew Files by Carolyn Keene (Pocket Books)
Titles such as *For Love or Money, The Stolen Kiss,* and *Hidden Meanings*

*Spy Girls by Elizabeth Cage (Pocket Books)
Titles such as *License to Thrill, Live and Let Spy,* and *Nobody Does It Better*

Horror

The Forbidden Game Series by L.J. Smith (Archway Paperbacks)
Titles such as *The Hunter, The Chase,* and *The Kill*

The Night World Series by L. J. Smith (Archway Paperbacks)
Titles such as *Night World: Secret Vampire* and *Night World: Spellbinder*

The Dark Visions Series by L. J. Smith (Archway Paperbacks)
Titles such as *The Strange Power, The Possessed,* and *The Passion*

The Fear Street Series by R. L. Stine (Archway Paperbacks)
Titles such as *Secret Admirer, The Boy Next Door,* and *The Confession*

The Cheerleader Series by R. L. Stine (Archway Paperbacks)
Titles such as *The First Evil, The Second Evil, The Third Evil,* and *The Evil Lives!*

The Fear Park Series by R. L. Stine (Archway Paperbacks)
Titles such as *The First Scream, The Loudest Scream,* and *The Last Scream*

The Super Chiller Series by R. L. Stine (Archway Paperbacks)
Titles such as *Party Summer, Goodnight Kiss,* and the *New Year's Party*

The Fear Street Sagas by R. L. Stine (Archway Paperbacks)
Titles such as *The Hidden Evil, House of Whispers,* and *The Betrayal*

Buffy, the Vampire Slayer Series by Christopher Golden and Nancy Holder (Pocket Books)
Titles such as *The Harvest, Angel Chronicles,* and *Blooded*

Extreme Zone by M. C. Sumner (Pocket Books)
Titles such as *Unseen Power, Night Terrors,* and *Dark Lies*

The Last Vampire Series by Christopher Pike (Pocket Books)
Titles such as *The Last Vampire, Black Blood, Red Dice,* and *Phantom*

*Passages to Suspense by Anne Schraff (Perfection Learning Corporation)
Titles such as *A Deadly Obsession; The Frozen Face; Like Father, Like Son; New Kid in Class;* and *Rage of the Tiger*

Sports

*Greats Series (New Readers Press)
Titles such as *Great Baseball of the 20th Century, Great Fights of the 20th Century, Great Football of the 20th Century*

*Millbrook Sports World by Bill Gutman (Millbrook Press)
Titles such as *Jim Abbott, Juan Gonzalez, Grant Hill, Larry Johnson, Shaquille O'Neal, Emmitt Smith, Jennifer Capriati, Tara Lipinsky, Tiger Woods,* and *Ken Griffey*

*New Wave Series by Mark Stewart (Millbrook Press)
Titles such as *Alex Rodriguez, Derek Geter, Tim Duncan,* and *Terrell Davis*

Classics

*Easy Classics (EMC Corporation)
Titles such as *Great Expectations, One Grave Too Many, Treasure Island, The Happy Prince, Rip Van Winkle,* and *Tom Sawyer*

*Retold Classics (Perfection Learning Corporation)
Titles such as *Retold American Classics, Retold British Classics, Retold Classic Myths, Retold World Myths, Retold American Classic Nonfiction,* and *Retold World Classics*

Anthologies

*Short stories by Dianne Swenson (Perfection Learning Corporation)
Titles such as *The Day Dad Cried and Other Stories, The Well-Kept Secret And Other Stories,* and *An Ended Friendship and Other Stories*

*Short stories by Robert Vitarelli (Perfection Learning Corporation)
Titles such as *Fire and Other Short Stories, Faces of the Dead and Other Short Stories,* and *Off the Hook and Other Short Stories*

*Fastback Series (Simon and Schuster)
Horror, Sports, Spy, Romance, Mystery, Crime and Detection

*Double Fastback Series (Simon and Schuster)
Horror, Sports, Spy, Romance, Mystery, S.O.S.

Read-Along Books and Tapes

Unabridged Read-alongs on Cassette Tapes (Listening Library, Inc.)
Titles such as *Great American Short Stories*, *Visions (Nineteen Short Stories by Outstanding Writers for Young Adults)*, *Award Winning Science Fiction*, *Sixteen (Short Stories by Outstanding Writers for Young Adults)*, and *American Humor and Satire*

*Theme-Related Listening and Reading (Listening Library, Inc.)
Titles such as *The Boxcar Children* by Gertrude Chandler Warner, *The Kid Who Only Hit Homers* by Matt Christopher, *The View from Saturday* by El Konigsburg, and *How to Fight a Girl* by Thomas Rockwell

*The Encounters Series by John Ibbitson, Paul Kropp, Donald Carline, and Martin Godfrey (EMC Publishing)
Titles such as *Amy's Wish*, *Burn Out*, *Dirt Bike*, *Gang Wars*, *Ice Hawk*, *Spin Out*, and *The Wimp*

*Pacemaker Classics—Edited Read-along Books/Tapes (Simon and Schuster)
Titles such as *The Call of the Wild*, *Treasure Island*, *Jane Eyre*, *Moby Dick*, and *The Moonstone*

*Fastback Read-along Books/Tapes (Simon and Schuster)
Titles such as *The Diary*, *The Disappearing Man*, *Night Games*, *Dressed Up for Murder*, *The Lottery Winner*, and *No Power on Earth*

Publishing Company Information

Aladdin Paperbacks (An Imprint of Simon and Schuster; see Simon and Schuster)

Archway Paperbacks (Distributed by Simon and Schuster; see Simon and Schuster)

Ballantine Books (Distributed by Random House, Inc.; see Random House, Inc.)

Bantam Double Day Dell (Corporate Office)
A Division of Random House
1540 Broadway
New York City, New York 10036
(800) 223-6834
(800) 323-9872 for title availability

Berkley Books (Distributed by Penguin-Putnam; see Penguin-Putnam)

EMC Paradigm
875 Montreal Way
St. Paul, Minnesota 55102
(651) 290-2800
(800) 328-1452

HarperCollins Publishers (Corporate Office)
10 East 53rd Street
New York City, New York 10022
For individual orders:
P.O. Box 588
Scranton, Pennsylvania 18512
(800) 331-3761
For school orders:
1000 Keystone Industrial Park
Scranton, Pennsylvania 18512
(800) 242-7737

Listening Library, Inc.
One Park Avenue
Old Greenwich, Connecticut 06870-1727
(800) 243-4504

The Millbrook Press
2 Old New Milford Road
Brookfield, Connecticut 06804
(203) 740-2220
(800) 462-4703

National Geographic Society
P.O. Box 60001
Tampa, Florida 33660
(800) 647-5463

New Readers Press
P.O. Box 888
Syracuse, New York 13210
(800) 448-8878

Penguin-Putnam
   1 Grosset Drive
   Kirkwood, New York 13795
   (800) 872-6657

Perfection Learning Corporation
   1000 N. Second Avenue
   Logan, Iowa 51546
   (712) 644-2831
   (800) 831-4190

Pocket Books (Distributed by Simon and Schuster; see Simon and Schuster)

Random House, Incorporated (Corporate Office)
   201 E. 50th Street
   New York, New York 10022
   (for information about authors)

Random House, Incorporated (Distribution Center)
   400 Hahn Road
   Westminster, Maryland 21157
   (For ordering information)
For individual orders:
   (800) 733-3000
For school orders:
   (800) 726-0600

Scholastic, Incorporated (Corporate Office)
   555 Broadway
   New York City, New York 10012
   (888) 307-1555

Scholastic, Incorporated (Customer Service)
   2931 E. McCarty Street
   Jefferson City, Missouri 65101
   (800) 724-6527

Simon and Schuster (Corporate Office)
   1230 Avenue of the Americas
   New York, New York 10020

Simon and Schuster (Customer Operations)
    100 Front Street
    Riverside, New Jersey 08075
    (800) 223-2336 (individual or school orders)

Aladdin Paperbacks
    (Orders: (212) 698-2711)

Pocket Books
    (Orders: (212) 698-7669)

Weekly Reader Corporation
    Executive and Editorial Offices
    245 Long Hill Road
    PO Box 2791
    Middletown, Connecticut 06457-9291

Catalogues: Books for Older Readers

Alta ESL Resource Center

Alta Book Center
    14 Adrian Court
    Burlingame, California 94010
    (800) ALTA/ESL
    fax (800) ALTA/FAX
    http://www.altaesl.com

Discovery Enterprises, Ltd.
    31 Laurelwood Drive
    Carlisle, Massachusetts 01741
    (800) 729-1720
    fax (978) 287-5402

Jamestown Publishers
    A Division of NTC/ Contemporary Publishing Company
    4255 West Touhy Avenue
    Lincolnwood, Illinois 60646-1975
    (800) 621-1918 Ext.305
    fax (800) 998-3103
    ntcpub@tribune.com
    http://www.jamestownpublishers.com

Listening Library
Unabridged Audiobooks for All Ages
One Park Avenue
Old Greenwich, Connecticut 06870-1727
(800) 243-4504
fax (800) 454-0606
http://www.listeninglib.com

New Readers Press
U.S. Publishing Division of Laubach Literacy
Department S99
P.O. Box 888
Syracuse, New York 13210-0888
(800) 448-8878
fax (315) 422-5561

Peachtree Publishers
494 Armour Circle, NE
Atlanta, Georgia 30324-4088
(800) 241-0113
fax (800) 875-8909
http://www.peachtree-online.com

Penguin Children's Books
A member of Penguin Putnam Inc.
A Pearson Company
Dial-Dutton-Viking-Warne
375 Hudson Street
New York, New York 10014
(212) 366-2000
fax (212) 366-2020
http://www.penguinputnam.com

Perfection Learning Corporation
1000 North Second Avenue
PO Box 500
Logan, Iowa 51546-1099
(800) 831-4190
fax (712) 644-2392
Perflern@netins.net

Puffin Books
  A member of Penguin Putnam, Inc.
  A Pearson Company
  375 Hudson Street
  New York, New York 10014
  (212) 366-2000
  fax (212) 366-2020
  http://www.penguinputnam.com

Putnam Children's Books
  A member of Penguin Putnam, Inc.
  GP Putnam's Sons-Philomel Books-PaperStar Books
  375 Hudson Street
  New York, New York 10014
  (212) 366-2480
  fax (212) 366-2933
  http://www.penguinputnam.com

Scholastic Professional Books
  P.O. Box 7502
  Jefferson City, Missouri 65102
  (800) 724-6527
  fax (800) 223-4011

Sundance
  Middle School and High School
  Dept. 0503
  P.O. Box 1326
  Littleton, Massachusetts 01460
  (800) 343-8204
  fax (800) 456-2419
  http://www.sundancepub.com

Troll Communications
  Grades K–8
  100 Corporate Drive
  Mahwah, New Jersey 07430
  (800) 541-1097
  http://www.troll.com

Upstart
A Division of Highsmith, Inc.
W5527 Highway 106
P.O. Box 800
Fort Atkinson, Wisconsin 53538-0800
(800) 448-4887
fax (800) 448-5828

Appendix A
Studies Used in the SSR Analysis

Aranha, M. 1985. "Sustained Silent Reading Goes East." *The Reading Teacher* 39 (2): 214–17.

Cline, R., and Kretke, G. 1980. "An Evaluation of Long-term SSR in the Junior High School." *Journal of Reading* 23 (6): 503–06.

Collins, C. 1980. "Sustained Silent Reading Periods: Effect on Teachers' Behaviors and Students' Achievement." *The Elementary School Journal* 81 (2): 109–14.

Davis, F., and Lucas, J. 1971. "An Experiment in Individualized Reading." *The Reading Teacher* 24 (8): 737–43, 747.

Elley, W. 1991. "Acquiring Literacy in a Second Language: The Effect of Book-based Programs." *Language Learning* 41 (3): 375–411.

Elley, W., and Mangubhai, F. 1983. "The Impact of Reading on Second Language Learning." *Reading Research Quarterly* 19 (1): 53–67.

Evans, H., and Towner, J. 1975. "Sustained Silent Reading: Does it Increase Skills?" *The Reading Teacher* 29 (2): 155–56.

Everett, I. 1987. *Recreational Reading Effects on Reading Comprehension Achievement.* M.A. thesis. New Jersey: Kern College of New Jersey. (ERIC Document Reproduction Service No. ED 283 123)

Fader, D. 1976. *The New Hooked on Books.* New York: Berkeley Medallion Book, Berkeley Publishing Company.

Farrell, E. 1982. "SSR as the Core of a Junior High School Reading Program." *Journal of Reading* 1 (26): 48–51.

Greaney, V. 1970. "A Comparison of Individualized and Basal Reader Approaches to Reading Instruction." *The Irish Journal of Education* 4 (1): 19–29.

Hafiz, F., and Tudor, I. 1989. "Extensive Reading and the Development of Language Skills." *English Language Teaching Journal* 43 (1): 4–13.

Holt, S., and O'Tuel, F. 1989. "The Effect of Sustained Silent Reading and Writing on Achievement and Attitudes of Seventh and Eighth Grade Students Reading Two Years Below Grade Level." *Reading Improvement* 26 (4): 290–97.

Jenkins, M. 1957. "Self-selection in Reading." *The Reading Teacher* 11 (2): 84–90.

Kaminsky, D. 1992. "Improving Intermediate Grade Level ESL Students' Attitudes Toward Recreational Reading." Ed.D. Practicum. Florida: Nova University. (ERIC Document Reproduction Service No. ED 347 509)

Lai, F. 1993. "The Effect of a Summer Reader Course on Reading and Writing Skills." *System* 21 (1): 87–100.

Lawson, H. 1968. "Effects of Free Reading on the Reading Achievement of Sixth-Grade Pupils." In *Forging Ahead in Reading* ed. J. A. Figuerel, 501–4. Newark, DE: International Reading Association.

Manning, G., and Manning, M. 1984. "What Models of Recreational Reading Make a Difference?" *Reading World* 23 (4): 375–80.

Maynes, F. 1981. "Uninterrupted Sustained Silent Reading." *Reading Research Quarterly* 17 (1): 159–160.

Minton, M. 1980. "The Effect of Sustained Silent Reading upon Comprehension and Attitudes Among Ninth Graders." *Journal of Reading* 23 (6): 498–502.

Oliver, M. 1973. The Effect of High Intensity Practice on Reading Comprehension. *Reading Improvement* 10 (2): 16–18.

———. 1976. "The Effect of High Intensity Practice on Reading Achievement." *Reading Improvement* 13 (4): 226–28.

Petrimoulx, J. 1988. "Sustained Silent Reading in an ESL Class: A Study." Paper presented at the 22nd Annual Meeting of the Teachers of English to Speakers of Other Languages, Chicago, Illinois. (ERIC Document Reproduction Service No. ED 301 068)

Pfau, D. 1967. "Effects of Planned Recreational Reading Programs." *The Reading Teacher* 21 (1): 34–9.

Schon, I., Hopkins, K., and Vojir, C. 1984. "The Effects of Spanish Reading Emphasis on the English and Spanish Reading Abilities of Hispanic High School Students." *Bilingual Review* 11 (1): 33–9.

———. 1985. "The Effects of Special Reading Time in Spanish on the Reading Abilities and Attitudes of Hispanic Junior High School Students." *Journal of Psycholinguistic Research* 14 (1): 57–65.

Sperzel, E. 1948. "The Effect of Comic Books on Vocabulary Growth and Reading Comprehension." *Elementary English* 25 (2): 109–13.

Summers, E., and McClelland, V. 1982. "A Field-based Evaluation of Sustained Silent Reading in Intermediate Grades." *The Alberta Journal of Educational Research* 28 (2): 100–12.

Wiscont, J. 1990. *A Study of the Sustained Silent Reading Program for Intermediate Grade Students in the Pulaski, Wisconsin School District.* M.S. Thesis. Oshkosh, Wisconsin: University of Wisconsin. (ERIC Document Reproduction Service No. ED 323 520)

Wolf, A., and Mikulecky, L. 1978. "Effects of USSR and of Reading Skills Instruction on Changes in Secondary School Students' Reading Attitudes and Achievement." In the *27th Yearbook of the National Reading Conference*, ed. S. D. Pearson and J. Hanson, 226–28. Clemson, SC: National Reading Conference.

Appendix B
Results of Thirty-Two Free Reading Programs

Notes

C-SS   refers to reading comprehension, statistically significant.

A-SS   refers to positive attitude toward reading, statistically significant.

A-OBS   indicates that positive attitude toward reading was observed through non-statistically measured indicators.

NA   means that this variable was not part of the research design objective(s) for the given experimental group.

ESL   indicates that the given experimental group was composed of English as-a-subsequent-language students.

LOSS   indicates that statistically significant differences were found in favor of the comparison group.

An asterisk* indicates that Spanish reading comprehension and positive attitude toward Spanish reading were the dependent variables.

Elementary Level Studies:

STUDY	YR	ESL	GR	C-SS	A-SS	A-OBS
1. Aranha	1985	YES	4	YES	YES	NA
2. Collins	1980	NO	2–6	NO	NO	NA
3. Elley & Mangubhai						
E1	1983	YES	4–5	YES	NA	NA
E2	1983	YES	4–5	YES	NA	NA
4. Elley (Niue)	1991	YES	3	YES	NA	YES
5. Elley (Singapore)	1991	YES	1	YES	NA	YES

STUDY	YR	ESL	GR	C-SS	A-SS	A-OBS
6. Evans & Towner	1975	NO	4	NO	NA	NA
7. Greaney	1970	NO	6	NA	YES	NA
8. Jenkins	1957	NO	2	NA	NA	YES
9. Kaminsky	1992	YES	4–6	NA	NA	YES
10. Lawson:						
E1	1968	NO	6	NO	NA	YES
E2	1968	NO	6	LOSS	NA	YES
E3	1968	NO	6	LOSS	NA	YES
11. Manning & Manning:						
E1	1984	NO	4	NO	NO	NA
E2	1984	NO	4	YES	YES	NA
E3	1984	NO	4	NO	YES	NA
12. Maynes	1981	NO	2–6	NA	NA	NO
13. Oliver	1973	NO	4–6	NO	NA	NA
14. Oliver:						
E1	1976	NO	4–6	NO	NA	YES
E2	1976	NO	4–6	NO	NA	YES
15. Pfau	1967	NO	1	NO	YES	NA
16. Sperzel:						
E1	1948	NO	5	NO	NA	NA
E2	1948	NO	5	NO	NA	NA
17. Wiscont	1990	NO	4–6	NA	NA	YES

Middle School and Junior High Level Studies:

STUDY	YR	ESL	GR	C-SS	A-SS	A-OBS
18. Cline & Kretke	1980	NO	JH	NO	YES	NA
19. Davis & Lucas	1971	NO	7–8	NO	NA	YES
20. Everett	1987	NO	8	NO	NA	YES
21. Farrell	1982	NO	8	NA	NA	YES
22. Holt & O'Tuel	1989	NO	7–8	YES	YES	NA
23. Lai:						
E1	1993	YES	7–9	YES	NA	NA
E2	1993	YES	7–9	YES	NA	NA
E3	1993	YES	7–9	NO	NA	NA
*24. Schon et al.	1985	NO	7–8	NO	NO	NA

Middle School and Junior High Level Studies:

25. Summers & McClelland	1982	NO	5–7	NO	NO	NA
26. Wolf & Mikulecky	1978	NO	7	NO	NO	NA

Senior High Level Studies:

STUDY	YR	ESL	GR	C-SS	A-SS	A-OBS
27. Hafiz & Tudor	1989	YES	HS	YES	NA	NA
28. Minton	1980	NO	9	NA	NA	NO
*29. Schon et al. (Tempe)	1984	NO	9–12	NO	NO	NA
*30. Schon et al. (Chandler)	1984	NO	10–12	NO	NO	NA
31. Fader	1976	NO	HS	NA	NA	YES

College Level Studies:

STUDY	YR	ESL	GR	C-SS	A-SS	A-OBS
32. Petrimoulx	1988	YES	COL	NO	NA	YES

Appendix C

Percentages of Experimental Groups that Included the Identified Factors for Each Category of Success

Notes

C-SS   refers to reading comprehension, statistically significant.

A-SS   refers to positive attitude toward reading, statistically significant.

A-OBS   indicates that positive attitude toward reading was observed through non-statistically measured indicators.

A-SS & A-OBS   refers to a combination of these two categories.

ACC = Access; APP = appeal; ENV = conducive environment; ENC = encouragement; STR = staff training; NACC = non-accountability; FOL = follow-up activities; and DTIME = distributed time to read.

CATEGORY	ACC	APP	ENV	ENC	STR	NACC	FOL	DTIME
C-SS	100	90	100	90	60	80	60	100
A-SS	100	71	100	86	57	100	57	100
C-SS & A-SS	100	82	100	88	59	88	59	100
A-OBS	100	80	100	93	20	87	47	93
A-SS & A-OBS	100	77	100	91	32	91	50	95

Appendix D
Pilot Student Questionnaire

Name _____   Teacher _____   Period _____
Date _____

1. Have you ever taken a reading class before?   yes   no

2. Where did you attend school last semester?   _____

3. What ESL level were you in last semester?   _____

4. When did you first come to this class? (date)   _____

5. Do you read at home or outside of class?

   1) never   2) sometimes   3) often

6. Do you enjoy reading?

   1) not at all   2) a little   3) some   4) a lot

7. Where do you usually get the books you read in class?

   1) classroom   2) home   3) school/public library
   4) book store/book club   5) relatives/friends

8. If you read for pleasure, where do you usually get your books? (You may choose more than one answer.)

   1) classroom   2) book store   3) home   4) school library

   5) public library   6) friend/relative   7) book club

9. Have you read any reading materials TODAY OR YESTER-DAY that you didn't get from a classroom? (Choose only one answer.)

   1) no   2) yes, one thing   3) yes, more than one thing

10. Have you read any reading materials DURING THE LAST WEEK that you didn't get from a classroom? (Choose only one answer.)

    1) no   2) yes, one thing   3) yes, more than one thing

11. Do you feel that your reading has improved (gotten better) during this past semester? (Choose only one answer.)

    1) no, not at all   2) yes, some   3) yes, a lot

12. [If you marked yes (#2 or #3) to the question that you just answered, please answer the next question. If you marked no, please do NOT answer the next question.]

    In what way(s) do you feel you can read better? (You may choose more than one answer by circling the letters.)

    1) I can understand the textbooks better in my other classes.

    2) I can read books (or other materials) for pleasure more easily.

    3) I feel more capable of doing well on reading tests.

    4) I am more capable of translating reading for my parents.

    5) Other: _____

Appendix E
Pilot Study Results*

Table 1
Gains on the Stanford Diagnostic Reading Test

	RAW SCORE MEAN	GRADE EQUIV. MEAN	STANDARD DEVIATION
Pretest	33.612	3.742	2.359
Posttest	42.246	5.271	3.044

$(t = 10.916, df = 124, p < .001)$

Table 2
Enjoyment of Reading

	NOT AT ALL	A LITTLE	SOME	A LOT
Pretest	0	33	59	33
Posttest	0	5	62	58

$(Chisquare = 27.574, df = 2, p < .001)$

*Note. For all tables, the number of respondants (n) = 125

Table 3
Frequency of Outside Reading

	NEVER	SOMETIMES	OFTEN
Pretest	10	90	25
Posttest	2	72	51

(Chisquare = 27.574, df = 2, p < .001)

Table 4
Perceived Reading Improvement

	NOT MUCH	SOME	A LOT
Posttest	2	46	77

Table 5
Range of Reading Sources

	CLASS	HOME	LIBRARY	STORE/CLUB	FRIENDS/RELATIVES
Pretest	100	12	30	8	6
Posttest	55	23	60	31	18

Note. Students could choose more than one source.

Appendix F

Interest Inventory

Name: _____

Circle the things you like to read about:

   a. adventure
   b. foods
   c. science
   d. space
   e. travel
   f. real life situations
   g. history
   h. animals
   i. comedy
   j. sports
   k. famous persons
   l. health and exercise
  m. mysteries
   n. horror
   o. fantasy
   p. other:

What kinds of materials do you like?

   a. magazines
   b. comic books
   c. newspapers
   d. novels
   e. paperbacks
   f. encyclopedias
   g. textbooks
   h. "how to" guides
   i. diaries and letters
   j. speeches
   k. other:

If you like to read any special series books or materials, or books by a certain author, please add the information here.

Appendix G
Outside Pleasure Reading

Week of: _____

Monday, _____
Title _____
Author _____
Pages Read _____ to _____

Tuesday, _____
Title _____
Author _____
Pages Read _____ to _____

Wednesday, _____
Title _____
Author _____
Pages Read _____ to _____

Thursday, _____
Title _____
Author _____
Pages Read _____ to _____

Friday, _____
Title _____
Author _____
Pages Read _____ to _____

Saturday, _____
Title _____
Author _____
Pages Read _____ to _____

Sunday, _____
Title _____
Author _____
Pages Read _____ to _____

Parent's,
Relative's, or
Guardian's
Signature: _____

Date
Signed: _____

Appendix H
Reading Record

Name _____ Period _____ Week of _____

DATE	PAGES READ		TITLE	NO.	RESPONSE OR PREDICTION	STAMP
	FROM	TO				

Appendix I
Reading Responses

1. I like what I just read because . . .
2. The last event that occurred in this story was . . .
3. The part I read today was mostly about one character. This character is a(n) _____ kind of person.
4. So far, the antagonist (bad guy) in this story seems to be . . .
5. Today I learned something new. I learned that . . .
6. The newspaper or magazine article I read was about . . .
7. In the next part of my book, I predict that _____ will probably happen.
8. A prediction that I made earlier turned out to be right. I predicted that _____ would happen.
9. I'm not sure that I really like this magazine yet. The reason I am unsure is that . . .
10. I was surprised by what I read today. I thought it would be about _____, but it was about _____ instead.
11. I would like to read more articles like the one I just read. Next time I might choose an article about . . .
12. I would recommend this book or article to students who . . .
13. I admire what this character did because (or BUT) . . .
14. One new idea I learned is . . .
15. The main character so far seems to be _____ because . . .
16. I didn't understand what I read today because . . .
17. I will share this article/book with _____ because . . .
18. The reason I chose this book or article was because . . .
19. What I read today was fiction/nonfiction. I know this because . . .
20. What made this book/article funny was . . .
21. If I were the author, I would add . . .

22. If I could be a person from this story, I would be _____ because . . .
23. What I read doesn't make sense because . . .
24. A person who has a problem like mine to solve is _____ because . . .
25. The reading is getting exciting because . . .
26. This story is important to me because . . .
27. If I could, I would change the part about . . .
28. I enjoy _____ in this story.
29. I did/did not like the ending to the story because . . .
30. YOUR OWN RESPONSE . . .

Appendix J

Student Pretest/Posttest Questionnaires

Student Posttest Questionnaire

Name _____   Teacher _____   Period _____
Date _____

1. Have you ever taken a reading class before?   yes   no

2. Where did you attend school last semester?   _____

3. What ESL level were you in last semester?   _____

   (If you were in regular or sheltered English, who was your teacher?)

4. When did you first come to this class? (date)

5. Who is your reading teacher now?

6. What grade are you in?   9 10 11 12

7. How often do you read at home or outside of class just for pleasure? Reading for pleasure means just for enjoyment. (Choose only *one* answer.)

   1) never   2) sometimes   3) often   4) every day

Name _____   Teacher _____   Period _____
Date _____

8. TODAY or YESTERDAY, just for pleasure, I read: (You may choose more than one answer.)

    1) nothing   2) a magazine   3) a newspaper

    4) a comic book   5) a book/part   6) something else
                              of a book

9. DURING THE LAST WEEK, just for pleasure I read: (You may choose more than one answer.)

    1) nothing   2) a magazine   3) a newspaper

    4) a comic book   5) a book/part   6) something else
                              of a book

10. If you read for pleasure, where do you *usually* get materials? (You may choose more than one answer.)

    1) classroom   2) book store   3) home   4) school library

    5) public library   6) friend/relative   7) book club

11. Have you read any reading materials TODAY or YESTER-DAY that you *didn't get from a classroom?* (Choose only *one* answer.)

    1) no   2) yes, one thing   3) yes, more than one thing

12. Have you read any reading materials DURING THE LAST WEEK that you *didn't get from a classroom?* (Choose only *one* answer.)

    1) no   2) yes, one thing   3) yes, more than one thing

Name _____   Teacher _____   Period _____
Date _____

13. Do any of your adult relatives who live with you read for plea-
    sure? (Choose only *one* answer.)

    1) never   2) sometimes   3) often   4) every day

14. If an adult relative in your home reads for pleasure, in what
    language(s) does this person read? (Choose only *one* an-
    swer.)

    1) English   2) Other _____   3) English and Other _____

15. How many books or reading materials do you think there are
    in your home? (Choose only *one* answer.)

    1) none   2) 1–10   3) 11–20   4) 21–30   5) More than 30

Student Posttest Questionnaire

Name _____   Teacher _____   Period _____
Date _____

1. When did you first come to this class? (date)   _____

2. Who is your reading teacher now?   _____

3. What grade are you in?   9 10 11 12

4. What ESL level or English class will you be in *next* semester?

5. How often do you read at home or outside of class just for pleasure? Reading for pleasure means just for enjoyment. (Choose only *one* answer.)

    1) never   2) sometimes   3) often   4) every day

6. TODAY or YESTERDAY, just for pleasure, I read: (You may choose more than one answer.)

    1) nothing   2) a magazine   3) a newspaper
    4) a comic book   5) a book/part   6) something else
                      of a book

7. DURING THE LAST WEEK, just for pleasure I read: (You may choose more than one answer.)

    1) nothing   2) a magazine   3) a newspaper
    4) a comic book   5) a book/part   6) something else
                      of a book

8. If you read for pleasure, where do you *usually* get materials? (You may choose more than one answer.)

    1) classroom 2) book store 3) home 4) school library
    5) public library 6) friend/relative 7) book club

Name _____   Teacher _____   Period _____

Date _____

9. Have you read any reading materials TODAY or YESTER-DAY that you *didn't get from a classroom?* (Choose only *one* answer.)

   1) no   2) yes, one thing   3) yes, more than one thing

10. Have you read any reading materials DURING THE LAST WEEK that you *didn't get from a classroom?* (Choose only *one* answer.)

   1) no   2) yes, one thing   3) yes, more than one thing

11. Do you feel your reading has improved (gotten better) during this past semester? (Choose only *one* answer.)

   1) not at all   2) yes, some   3) yes, a lot

12. [If you marked yes (#2 or #3) to the question that you just answered, please answer the next question. *If you marked no, please do NOT answer the next question.*]

   In what way(s) do you feel you can read better? (You may choose more than one answer by circling the letters.)

   1) I can understand the textbooks better in my other classes.

   2) I can read books (or other materials) for pleasure more easily.

   3) I feel more capable of doing well on reading tests.

   4) I am more capable of translating reading for my parents.

   5) Other: _____

Appendix K
Pretest, Posttest, and Gain Score Means

Table 1
Stanford Diagnostic Reading Test (SDRT)

VAR	N	PRE	(SD)	POST	(SD)	GAIN	(SD)
1	131	26.66	(8.79)	35.37	(8.87)	8.71	(5.86)
2	117	29.71	(8.71)	36.75	(9.73)	7.04	(5.68)

Notes.
Var = school: 1 = home and 2 = community
SD = standard deviation

Table 2
Student Attitude Survey

VAR	N	PRE	(SD)	N	POST	(SD)	N	GAIN	(SD)
1	119	28.58	(5.79)	119	31.32	(4.97)	108	2.54	(5.05)
2	105	29.06	(5.25)	99	30.07	(5.06)	88	0.53	(4.35)

Notes.
Var = school: 1 = home and 2 = community
SD = standard deviation

Table 3
Separate Items on the Home School Student Attitude Survey

VARIABLE	PRE MEAN	POST MEAN	GAIN MEAN
1.	3.24	3.72	0.48
3.	3.78	3.87	0.09
4.	3.56	4.03	0.47
5.	2.70	3.22	0.52
6.	3.98	3.98	0.00
10.	3.94	4.12	0.18
11.	3.70	4.28	0.58
15.	3.67	4.09	0.42

Notes. Variables = item number on the Survey:

  1) Reading is for learning but not for enjoyment.

  3) Reading is a good way to spend spare time.

  4) Books are a bore.

  5) Watching TV is better than reading.

  6) Reading is rewarding to me.

10) There are many books which I hope to read.

11) Books should only be read when they are assigned.

15) Reading is boring.

Score represents a possible range of 1–5, with a 1 representing least positive attitude toward reading and a 5 representing the most positive.

Table 4
Separate Items on the Community School Attitude Survey

VARIABLE	PRE MEAN	POST MEAN	GAIN MEAN
1.	3.48	3.84	0.36
3.	3.77	3.99	0.22
4.	3.78	3.80	0.02
5.	2.82	3.05	0.23
6.	3.71	3.61	−0.10
10.	3.75	3.91	0.16
11.	3.98	3.88	−0.10
15.	3.75	4.04	0.29

Notes. Variable = item number on the Survey:
1) Reading is for learning but not for enjoyment.
3) Reading is a good way to spend spare time.
4) Books are a bore.
5) Watching TV is better than reading.
6) Reading is rewarding to me.
10) There are many books which I hope to read.
11) Books should only be read when they are assigned.
15) Reading is boring.

Score represents a possible range of 1–5, with a 1 representing least positive attitude toward reading and a 5 representing the most positive.

Table 5
Questionnaire: Frequency of Outside Pleasure Reading

VAR	N	PRE	(SD)	N	POST	(SD)	N	GAIN	(SD)
1.	117	2.34	(.70)	119	2.77	(.76)	107	0.43	(.75)
2.	105	2.70	(.83)	102	2.74	(.80)	92	−0.04	(.85)

Notes.
Var = school: 1 = home and 2 = community
SD = standard deviation

Table 6

Pretest and Posttest Totals of Students for Each "Frequency of Outside Pleasure Reading" Category

VARIABLE	N	1	2	3	4
1 Pre	117	5	77	25	10
1 Post	119	1	48	47	23
2 Pre	105	3	47	33	22
2 Post	102	2	43	37	20

Notes.
Categories: 1, never; 2, sometimes; 3, often; and 4, every day
Var = school: 1 = home and 2 = community

Table 7

Questionnaire: Wider Range of Pleasure Reading Sources

VAR	N	PRE	(SD)	N	POST	(SD)	N	GAIN	(SD)
1.	117	1.54	(.80)	119	2.27	(.98)	107	.73	(1.05)
2.	105	2.06	(1.04)	102	2.11	(1.24)	92	.09	(1.23)

Notes.
Var = school: 1 = home and 2 = community
SD = standard deviation

Table 8

Numbers of Total Reading Sources for Each School By Category

VARIABLE	N	1	2	3	4	5	6	7	TRes
1 PRE	117	43	16	55	9	32	19	4	(178)
1 POS	119	75	23	46	14	42	27	43	(270)
2 PRE	105	33	23	57	31	45	26	1	(216)
2 POS	102	37	27	45	36	42	23	5	(215)

Notes.
Var = school: 1 = home and 2 = community
PRE = pretest; POS = posttest
1 = classroom; 2 = bookstore; 3 = home; 4 = school library; 5 = public library; 6 = friend/relative; 7 = book club
TRes = Total Responses

Appendix L
Reader's Survey

Name: _____

Date: _____   Period: _____

Please complete the following survey thoughtfully, *using complete sentences. You will need more than one sentence to answer these questions.* As you answer the questions, think about ALL the reading you have done this year, not just the things you read in English. Think about reading for other subjects, reading for fun (yes, some of you do that), reading magazines, cards and letters, etc. Tell me what you really think. I know some of you have answered similar questions before, but you may find that your opinions have changed.

1. My earliest memory of reading, or being read to is (include as much information and description as you can remember) _____

_____

_____

_____

2. One memory about reading in school that sticks out in my mind is _____

_____

_____

_____

3. I think the best thing anybody could do to help a young child learn to read is

_____

_____

_____

4. The thing that surprised me about reading in high school is _____

_____

_____

_____

5. I think I would read more if (give reasons also) _____

_____

_____

_____

6. If I were a teacher, I would encourage students to read more by _____

_____

_____

_____

7. The most valuable thing about reading is _____

_____

_____

_____

8. In my family, people read because _____

_____

_____

_____

9. When I am a parent, I will tell my children the following about reading: ___

_____

_____

_____

10. If someone gave me a $50 gift certificate at Barnes & Noble I would buy (be very specific—picture the clerk ringing up your purchases) _____

_____

_____

11. If I were to write a novel, it would be about _____

_____

_____

_____

12. The differences between watching a story on TV and reading in a book are

_____

_____

_____

13. The best books and stories always _____

_____

_____

_____

14. If I could change one thing about my own reading it would be _____

_____

_____

_____

15. Use the bottom of this sheet and write me a letter. Tell me anything else you have to add on the subject of reading—why you love it or hate it, what might help you be a better reader, what are the best things to read, how should reading be taught—the subject is endless. Please write a complete page and don't forget to sign your name.

Signature: _____

Appendix M
Parent Survey

Name of Student: _____   Grade Level of Student:_____

1. Does your child read for pleasure at home in the evenings or on the weekends?

    not at all   some   a great deal

2. What topics does (s)he like to read about?

3. Do *you* read for pleasure at home? If so, what kinds of things do you usually read?

4. Do you ever have discussions with your child about what (s)he has been reading in school or outside of school?

5. When your child was younger, did you read aloud to him/her?

6. Does your child do any writing at home that is not part of his/her homework? Explain.

7. Do you ever help your child at home with writing assignments from school? Explain.

8. What kinds of writing do *you* do at home in the evenings and on the weekends? Does your child see you when you do this writing?

9. What would you like to see your child do as a reader or writer that you feel (s)he isn't doing now at all or as often as you'd like?

10. (A) Does your child think that it is important to read and write fluently? Explain.

    (B) Do you feel that it is important for your child to read and write fluently? Explain.

Appendix N
School Year Reading Log

Name _____ Grade _____

DATE COMPLETED	TITLE OF BOOK	AUTHOR

References

Allen, J. 1995. *It's Never too Late: Leading Adolescents to Lifelong Literacy*. Portsmouth, NH: Heinemann.

Allington, R. 1975. "Sustained Approaches to Reading and Writing." *Language Arts* 52 (6): 813–15.

Aranha, M. 1985. "Sustained Silent Reading Goes East." *The Reading Teacher* 39 (2): 214–17.

Atwell, N. 1987. *In the Middle: Writing, Reading, and Learning with Adolescents*. Portsmouth, NH: Heinemann.

Azabdaftari, B. 1992. *The Concept of Extensive Reading in the Light of L1-L2 Hypothesis*. Paper presented at the Twenty-Sixth Annual Meeting of the Teachers of English to Speakers of Other Languages, Vancouver, British Columbia, Canada. (ERIC Document Reproduction Service No. ED 250 864)

Barbe, W., and Abbott, J. 1975. *Personalized Reading Instruction: New Techniques that Increase Reading Skills and Comprehension*. West Nyack, NY: Parker Publishing Company, Inc.

Cardanelli, A. 1992. "Teachers under Cover: Promoting the Personal Reading of Teachers." *The Reading Teacher* 45 (9): 664–68.

Carlsen, G., and Sherrill, A. 1988. *Voices of Readers: How We Come to Love Books*. Urbana, IL: National Council of Teachers of English.

Chambers, A. 1996. *The Reading Environment: How Adults Help Children Enjoy Books*. York, ME: Stenhouse Publishers.

Cho, K. S., and Krashen, S. 1994. "Acquisition of Vocabulary from the Sweet Valley Kids Series; Adult ESL Acquisition." *Journal of Reading* 37 (8): 662–67.

Clary, L. 1991. "Getting Adolescents to Read." *Journal of Reading* 34 (5): 340–45.

Cline, R., and Kretke, G. 1980. "An Evaluation of Long-term SSR in the Junior High School." *Journal of Reading* 23 (6): 503–6.

Constantino, R. 1998. "I Did Not Know You Could Get Such Things There! Secondary ESL Students' Understanding, Use and Beliefs Concerning the School and Public Library." In *Literacy, Access, and Libraries Among the Language Minority Population*, ed. R, Constantino, 53–67. Lanham, MD: Scarecrow Press.

Cronbach, Lee J. 1971. *Essentials of Psychological Testing* (3rd Ed.). NY: Harper and Brothers.

Davis, L. 1992. "Principals Serve Well as Reading Role Models." *Curriculum Review* 32 (3): 18.

Davis, F., and Lucas, J. 1971. "An Experiment in Individualized Reading." *The Reading Teacher* 24 (8): 737–43, 747.

Dorrell, L., and Carroll, E. 1981. "Spider-Man at the Library." *School Library Journal* 27: 17–19.

Elley, W. 1991. "Acquiring Literacy in a Second Language: The Effect of Book-based Programs." *Language Learning* 41 (3): 375–411.

———— 1992. *How in the World do Students Read?* Hamburg, Germany: The International Association for the Evaluation of Educational Achievement.

Elley, W., and Mangubhai, F. 1983. "The Impact of Reading on Second Language Learning." *Reading Research Quarterly* 19 (1): 53–67.

Everett, I. 1987. *Recreational Reading Effects on Reading Comprehension Achievement.* M.A. thesis. NJ: Kern College of New Jersey. (ERIC Document Reproduction Service No. ED 283 123)

Fader, D. 1976. *The New Hooked on Books.* NY: Berkeley Medallion Book, Berkeley Publishing Company.

Farrell, E. 1982. "SSR as the Core of a Junior High School Reading Program." *Journal of Reading* 1 (26): 48–51.

Gallo, D. 1968. "Free Reading and Book Reports: An Informal Survey of Grade Eleven." *Journal of Reading* 11 (7): 532–38.

Gambrell, L. 1978. "Getting Started with Sustained Silent Reading and Keeping it Going." *The Reading Teacher* 32 (3):, 328–31.

Ganz, P., and Theofield, M. 1974. "Suggestions for Starting SSR." *Journal of Reading* 17 (8): 614–16.

Gradman, H., and Hanania, E. 1992. "The Relative Importance of Reading for Language Learning Programs." In *Quilt and Quill: Achieving and Maintaining Quality in Language Teaching and Learning,* ed. J. Harris, 431–41. Hong Kong: Education Department, Institute of Language in Education.

Greaney, V. 1970. "A Comparison of Individualized and Basal Reader Approaches to Reading Instruction." *The Irish Journal of Education* 4 (1): 19–29.

Greaney, V., and Clarke, M. 1975. "A Longitudinal Study of the Effects of Two Reading Methods on Leisure-time Reading Habits." In *Reading: What of the future?*, ed. D. Moyle, 107–14. London: United Kingdom Reading Association.

Hafiz, F., and Tudor, I. 1989. "Extensive Reading and the Development of Language Skills." *English Language Teaching Journal* 43 (1): 4–13.

Heathington, B. 1979. "What To Do About Reading Motivation and the Middle School." *Journal of Reading* 22 (8): 709–13.

Holt, S., and O'Tuel, F. 1989. "The Effect of Sustained Silent Reading and Writing on Achievement and Attitudes of Seventh and Eighth Grade Students Reading Two Years Below Grade Level." *Reading Improvement* 26 (4): 290–97.

Hunt, L. 1967. Evaluation Through Teacher-pupil Conferences. In *The Evaluation of Children's Reading Achievement*, ed. T. C. Barrett, 111–26. Newark, DE: International Reading Association.

Jenkins, M. 1957. "Self-selection in Reading." *The Reading Teacher* 11 (2): 84–90.

Jones, C. 1978. "20 Minute Vacations." *Journal of Reading* 22 (2): 102.

Kaminsky, D. 1992. *Improving Intermediate Grade Level ESL Students' Attitudes Toward Recreational Reading*. Ed.D. Practicum. Florida: Nova University. (ERIC Document Reproduction Service No. ED 347 509).

Kohn, A. 1993. *Punished by Rewards*. Boston: Houghton-Mifflin.

———. 1998. "What to look for in a Classroom . . . and Other Essays." San Francisco, CA: Jossey-Bass Publishers.

Krashen, S. 1987. "Encouraging Free Reading." In *Fifty-First Yearbook of the Claremont Reading Conference*, ed. M. Douglas, 1–10. Claremont, California: Claremont Graduate School.

———. 1988. "Do We Learn to Read by Reading? The Relationship Between Free Reading and Reading Ability." In *Linguistics in Context: Connecting Observation and Understanding*, ed. D. Tannen, 269–298. Norwood, NJ: Ablex.

———. 1993. *The Power of Reading*. Englewood, Colorado: Libraries Unlimited.

———. 1996. "Is Free Reading Always Easy Reading?" *California English* 1 (3): 23.

Krashen, S., and McQuillan, J. 1996. *The Case for Late Intervention: Once a Good Reader, Always a Good Reader*. Culver City, CA: Language Education Associates.

Lai, F. 1993. "The Effect of a Summer Reader Course on Reading and Writing Skills." *System* 21 (1): 87–100.

Leonhardt, M. 1996. *Keeping Kids Reading: How to Raise Avid Readers in the Video Age*. NY: Crown Publishers.

———. 1997. *99 Ways to Get Kids to Love Reading and 100 Books They'll Love*. NY: Three Rivers Press.

Lawson, H. 1968. "Effects of Free Reading on the Reading Achievement of Sixth-grade Pupils." In *Forging Ahead in Reading*, ed. J. A. Figurel, 501–4. Newark, DE: International Reading Association.

Mangubhai, F., and Elley, W. 1982. "The Role of Reading in Promoting ESL." *Language, Learning, and Communication* 1 (2): 151–60.

Manning, G., and Manning, M. 1984. "What Models of Recreational Reading Make a Difference?" *Reading World* 23 (4): 375–80.

Manning-Dowd, A. 1985. *The Effectiveness of SSR: A Review of the Research*. Information Analysis (Report No. CS 008 607). (ERIC Document Reproduction Service No. ED 276 970)

Maynes, F. 1981. "Uninterrupted Sustained Silent Reading." *Reading Research Quarterly* 17 (1): 159–60.

McCracken, R. 1971. "Initiating Sustained Silent Reading." *Journal of Reading* 14 (8): 521–24, 582–83.

McCracken, R., and McCracken, M. 1978. "Modeling Is the Key to Sustained Silent Reading." *The Reading Teacher* 31 (4): 406–8.

McQuillan, J. 1997. "The Effects of Incentives on Reading." *Reading Research and Instruction* 46 (2): 111–25.

Moffitt, M., and Wartella, E. 1992. "Youth and Reading: A Survey of Leisure Reading Pursuits of Female and Male Adolescents." *Reading Research and Instruction* 31 (2): 1–17.

Moore, C., Jones, C., and Miller, D. 1980. "What We Know After a Decade of Sustained Silent Reading." *The Reading Teacher* 33 (4): 445–50.

Mork, T. 1972. "Sustained Silent Reading in the Classroom." *The Reading Teacher* 25 (5): 438–41.

Morrow, L. 1982. "Relationships Between Literature Programs, Library Corner Designs, and Children's Use of Literature." *Journal of Educational Research* 75: 339–44.

Odean, K. 1997. *Great Books for Girls: More than 600 Books to Inspire Today's Girls and Tomorrow's Women.* NY: Ballantine Books.

Oliver, M. 1970. "High Intensity Practice: The Right to Enjoy Reading." *Education* 91 (1), 69–71.

———. 1973. "The Effect of High Intensity Practice on Reading Comprehension." *Reading Improvement* 10 (2): 16–18.

———. 1976. The Effect of High Intensity Practice on Reading Achievement. *Reading Improvement* 13 (4): 226–28.

O'Masta, G., and Wolf, J. 1991. "Encouraging Independent Reading Through the Reading Millionaires' Project." *The Reading Teacher* 44 (9): 656–62.

Pearson, D., and Stephens, D. 1994. "Learning About Literacy: A 30-Year Journey." In *Theoretical Models and Processes of Reading*, ed. R. Ruddell, M. Ruddell, and H. Singer, 22–42. Newark, DE: International Reading Association.

Petre, R. 1971. "Reading Breaks Make it in Maryland." *Journal of Reading* 15 (3): 191–94.

Petrimoulx, J. 1988. *Sustained Silent Reading in an ESL Class: A Study.* Paper presented at the 22nd Annual Meeting of the Teachers of English to Speakers of Other Languages, Chicago, Illinois. (ERIC Document Reproduction Service No. ED 301 068)

Pfau, D. 1967. "Effects of Planned Recreational Reading Programs." *The Reading Teacher* 21 (1): 34–39.

Pucci, S. 1998. "Supporting Spanish Language Literacy: Latino Children and School and Community Libraries." In *Literacy, Access, and Libraries Among the Language Minority Population*, ed. R. Constantino, 17–52. Lanham, MD: Scarecrow Press.

Ramos, F., and Krashen, S. 1998. "The Impact of One Trip to the Public Library: Making Books Available May Be the Best Incentive for Reading." *The Reading Teacher* 51 (7): 614–15.

Reed, A. 1988. *Comics to Classics: A Parent's Guide to Books for Teens and Preteens.* Newark, DE: International Reading Association.

Russikoff, K., and Pilgreen, J. 1994. "Shaking the Tree of 'Forbidden Fruit': A Study of Light Reading." *Reading Improvement* 31 (2): 122–23.

Sadoski, M. 1980. "Ten Years of Uninterrupted Sustained Silent Reading." *Reading Improvement* 17 (2): 153–56.

Sanacore, J. 1992. "Encouraging the Lifetime Reading Habit." *Journal of Reading* 35 (6): 474–77.

Sartain, H. 1960. "The Roseville Experiment with Individualized Reading." *The Reading Teacher*, 13: 277–81.

Sherman, M. J. 1996. "Free Choice Reading? Are You Kidding?" In *More Teens' Favorite Books: Young Adults Choices 1993–1995*. Newark, DE: International Reading Association.

Smith, F. 1988a. *Understanding Reading*. Hillsdale, NJ: Lawrence Erlbaum Associates, Inc.

———. 1988b. *Joining the Literacy Club: Further Essays into Education*. Portsmouth, NH: Heinemann.

Trelease, J. 1995. *The Read-aloud Handbook*. NY: Penguin Books.

Tse, L., and McQuillan, J. 1998. "Changing Reading Attitudes: The Power of Bringing Books into the Classroom". In *Literacy, Access, and Libraries Among the Language Minority Population*, ed. R. Constantino, 193–208. Lanham, MD: Scarecrow Press.

Ujiie, J., and Krashen, S. 1996. "Is Comic Book Reading Harmful? Comic Book Reading, School Achievement, and Pleasure Reading Among Seventh Graders." *CSLA Journal* 19 (2): 27–28.

Vandevier, R. 1992. "Parents Take the Pledge to Keep Their Children Reading at Home. *Curriculum Review* 32 (4):19.

Van Jura, S. 1984. "Secondary Students at Risk: Two Giant Steps Toward Independence in Reading." *Journal of Reading* 27 (6):, 540–43.

Von Sprecken, D., and Krashen, S. 1998. "Do Students Read During Sustained Silent Reading?" *The California Reader* 32 (1): 11–13.

Watkins, M., and Edwards, V. 1992. "Extracurricular Reading and Reading Achievement: The Rich Stay Rich and the Poor Don't Read." *Reading Improvement* 29: 236–42.

Wheldall, K., and Entwhisle, J. 1988. "Back in the USSR: The Effect of Teacher Modelling of Silent Reading on Pupils' Reading Behaviour in the Primary School Classroom." *Educational Psychology* 8: 51–56.

Wiscont, J. 1990. *A Study of the Sustained Silent Reading Program for Intermediate Grade Students in the Pulaski, Wisconsin School District*. M.S. Thesis. Oshkosh, Wisconsin: University of Wisconsin. (ERIC Document Reproduction Service No. ED 323–520)

Index

DATE DUE
